SABBATICAL

KERIE SEAMANS

CONTENTS

This book is dedicated to those that lost their lives during the Covid-19 pandemic and those that mourn them.

FOREWORD

You don't hear about Americans taking sabbaticals too often. Maybe faculty members, but not your average thirty-something woman. It's just not a thing in America. So, you can imagine that when I decided to quit my job in Corporate Finance and 'go traveling,' people thought I was nuts.

Women seem to be particularly inspired by my journey. While men are also inspired, I find that more often than not, they think I'm crazy. I consider 'my trip,' as I've come to call it, to be one of the most defining parts of my life and I enjoy talking about it more than I enjoy talking about my vocation (I prefer speaking of VA-cation over VO-cation). My tale often instills a sense of awe and elicits reactions that run the gamut from wonder and excitement to confusion and shock. I hope that this story inspires you to execute your own journey, whatever that may be. So, here goes . . .

At the ripe age of thirty-two years old, I quit my corporate job and bought a one-way ticket from Boston to South America. Equipped with a strategically packed backpack, a guidebook for my first country, and a generous supply of sunscreen, I boarded a plane bound for Buenos Aires,

Argentina. I was a solo, blonde ("Rubia! Rubia!") American woman and I was ready to tackle Latin America.

It took some guts to make this decision and follow through with it, although I realize that more in hindsight than I did at the time. Admittedly, I was terrified about giving up my job and the nice salary that came along with it. Not to mention my apartment, car, and all of the other material things in my life that I had become accustomed to. More importantly, there were my friends, family, and lover(s). What would they think of this? Would they be waiting for me when I came back? What if I didn't come back? The questions were endless . . .

I had been in a love hate relationship with Corporate America for over a decade. I could never fully embrace the fact that someone else dictated my schedule, how much time I could take off, and when I could take that time off. It nagged at me over the years and I began to feel like a caged animal. To try to combat these feelings, I made changes—in no particular order, I went back to school to get a graduate degree, I changed companies, I relocated, and I started practicing yoga. Nothing could take away the feeling that someone else was running my life.

My resentment built and fed itself until I became your classic, miserable nine-to-five who really only enjoyed outside of work time. Each morning, I would wake up and roll my eyes before getting ready to head into the office for the daily grind. I realized that I had to make a drastic change in order to fulfill my ideals of freedom and simplicity.

I had developed the travel bug during my twenties, and I have Corporate America to thank in part for that. At the age of twenty-three, I relocated to London, working for a year at a subsidiary of my large American company. Before this big move, I did not even have a passport! In the past, US citizens could travel to Canada and Mexico without one, and considering I had never been overseas, I had no reason to acquire a passport. As a kid, my family and I would take short domestic trips and in college, I traveled to California a few times, but that was about it.

Because of my lack of experience abroad, my company was hesitant to send me to London alone. However, the team there had selected me during the interview process and I assured everyone that I would be just fine. What a fantastic year it was! While I worked of course, I also spent much of my free time traveling throughout Europe, hopping on cheap flights to spend weekends in other cities. Occasionally I traveled with a buddy, but I visited many places independently, falling in love with solo travel. I was enamored by every place I visited and constantly desired to see and experience more.

Returning to Boston after my year abroad, I proceeded to torment myself for approximately six years, constantly wondering how I could be living my life differently. I had learned so much about other cultures and had come to covet many European ways, a big one being the propensity to travel long term and not be looked down upon.

During the short trips I had taken in my life, I met several 'long-term travelers.' I found their stories to be so interesting and I envied their paths forward as they continued their journeys with no real plan while I went home to my strict, routine life. I found myself thinking about these long-term travelers all the time. A very close friend of mine was in a similar situation to me (tormenting herself about the nine-to-five, debating the long-term travel thing, etc.) and she ultimately pulled the trigger and traveled through Asia for several months. This was inspiring and to put it bluntly, helped to ignite the fire under my ass.

I recognized that there would never be a perfect time to ditch the nine-to-five and travel the world. I could get hit by a bus while I was waiting for that perfect time, or more likely, die of skin cancer that consistently threatened my ginger complexion. I could wait until I saved X amount of money, or until after this wedding or that baby shower, but I finally decided that I didn't want to wait any longer. I was young(ish), healthy, single(ish), and childless (the latter two of which I had been ostracized for like most single American women in their thirties). I couldn't have been more free than I was! So, I made my decision and began the preparations. Was I kind of nervous? Yes, of course. Was I the most excited about something than I had ever been in my life? Most definitely.

"Why do you want to go traveling on a rice, beans, and hostel budget when you have such a nice lifestyle in Boston?" people wondered. "Won't you be lonely or afraid?" they asked. "Why not buy a condo instead?" they continued. "Are you going ALONE? Are you crazy?!?!" they exclaimed. I didn't let them faze me, knowing that I felt most alive while I was traveling, and that experiences were and always would be much more valuable to me than material things.

My friends would joke that I was born into the wrong century, that I had a sense of idealism that did not fit with modern culture. They were right in many ways—I did not seek normalcy, had an ever-present longing, and craved constant excitement and change. A classic overthinker, I was unfulfilled, constantly wondering how to make my place in this world more meaningful. Once I made my decision to travel, I couldn't wait to get out of my comfort zone and meet awesome new people with whom I would make lifelong memories. I mean, that was totally going to happen —right?!?!

The ending to this story should be fairly obvious—while fraught with challenges, the six months I spent traveling through South and Central America were some of the best of my entire life. I have no regrets and would make the same decision again if given the same circumstances.

I hiked glaciers, trekked through jungles, communicated in a new language, learned to tango, slept in hammocks, swam with sharks, walked with penguins, found love, contemplated the use of psychedelic drugs, and developed lifelong friendships. I was bitten by bed bugs, got lost in new cities, took grimy 24-hour bus rides, was involved in a boat crash, and got used to hearing the catcall 'Rubia! Rubia!' hollered by local men. While I didn't go into the journey with goals of taking risks and challenging myself, I ultimately did so and became proud of my feats.

I developed a deep appreciation of the things I took for granted (I'm literally talking food, shelter, and water) and what was ultimately important and valuable in life. I developed the utmost respect for native peoples, their cultures, successes, challenges, and deep family values. I bonded with other travelers, particularly other solo women travelers, from all over the world.

To this day, when I mention I traveled through South America solo for six months, the first question I always get is, "YOU DID THAT ALONE?!?!?!?!!?" It still tickles me every time . . .

Names have been changed throughout the story to protect the innocent

To view photos of my journey, follow gone_on_sabbatical on Instagram

1

THE DECISION

In 2014, at the age of thirty-two, I decided to quit my finance job in Corporate America and move to South America temporarily. "How long is temporarily?" people asked. I responded with, "It depends."

It depended on how much money I could save before I departed and how long I could make that money last. I was thinking three months minimum, six months maximum. Taking a sabbatical like this had been on my mind for years. Most people thought it was crazy, while many people thought it was great. I was of both minds, but erred on the side of greatness. You Only Live Once (YOLO!), as they say.

At the time of my decision, I had been doing a great deal of thinking (or torturing myself to put it more accurately) about how society defines success and happiness vs. what truly makes one successful and happy. In America, people care so much about money, status, other peoples' opinions, and keeping up with the Joneses. I grew up with a definition of success not unlike many others'—go to college, get a good job, climb the Corporate ladder, and keep making more money in order to buy more and better things.

That was the path I'd taken until my thirty second year, and it had served me well in many ways. However, I was troubled by the vision of my future self in a sterile office environment, pressured by unceasing deadlines and office politics and bored to tears with the work I was doing. I couldn't help but constantly think of those long-term travelers I had met during my brief vacations and how much I envied them. I needed to put the torment to a stop and realize my dream.

I wasn't planning to banish myself from Corporate America for life. Obviously, I needed to make a living and had invested a great deal of time and energy in my education. I didn't want to throw away all of my hard work and let my brain go idle. I just needed to get some exploring out of my system and figure out where I wanted to land upon my return; I needed to do some soul-searching if you will.

When I made the decision to go traveling, I was a Finance Manager at a Fortune 1000 company that will remain nameless for reasons that will soon become obvious. As far as the aforementioned American definition of success goes, I was doing well—earning a respectable salary, putting my brain to use in my field of study, living in the city, indulging in expensive cocktails and trips on the weekends, etcetera, etcetera.

There was a big problem though—frankly, I did not like my job. It was a stressful grind and I felt overworked and underappreciated. I hated how people in the office thought it was novel that I took all of my vacation time, and even more so that I would take two weeks at a time to travel to remote destinations. I loathed the fact that once I took those two weeks, I was pretty much stuck in cubicle hell for the remainder of the year with no permitted escape. I schemed about taking sick days to add to my vacation time, but couldn't bring myself to do it because it felt too dishonest.

My personal life was a bit complicated during this time. While I was not in a serious relationship, I was involved in a forbidden workplace love. It was your classic, unexpected romance developed over long days at the office. Contrary to the classic storyline, however, there was no fairy tale ending in the cards. My forbidden lover and I were at very different points in our lives (no, he was not married) and worked too closely together for a personal relationship to ever work out.

It's funny to look back now and think about our big secret —in hindsight I think, who in the world did we think we were kidding?!?! I digress . . . the point is, I had fallen for a colleague with whom my relationship was a big Corporate No-No.

I was also casually dating 'guys I should be dating' (nice, successful, age-appropriate men who looked great on paper). None of these guys were sparking my long-term interest though. So, to recap: I hated my job, I was simultaneously participating in an inappropriate relationship and boring, dead end relationships, and I had been yearning to travel long term. While the fact that I had feelings for my colleague complicated my decision to leave, I knew that it would be best for everyone in the long run if I did just that. The timing seemed ideal—no more prolonging the inevitable as it ate me up inside.

There were some other factors that pushed me in the nomadic direction. Unlike most single women my age, I did not feel the societal, family, personal, or peer pressure to settle down, get married, and have babies. I was also fortunate enough to not have any student loans (no, my family is not rich; I funded my education entirely through scholarships).

This lack of a committed relationship, children, and debt put me in a good position to disappear for a while. I wasn't running away (or was I?! I didn't know). While I was not sure what I was setting out to find, I knew it was something that I needed.

As I've already mentioned, people had lots of questions when I started to spread the news. One question that I heard frequently was "Why South America?" There were many reasons. One was that I had never been to South America and I was very interested in broadening my horizons. South America is home to a vast variety of beautiful places and fascinating things that called to me.

In fact, being the Type-A person that I was, I started to make important, yet initially haphazard, lists like the following:

- Glaciers—Patagonia
- Wildlife—Amazon Rainforest
- Cosmopolitan Latin city—Buenos Aires
- Best malbec in the world—Mendoza
- The Andes
- Must see: Machu Picchu
- Learn Spanish

In addition to seeing and doing cool things, I wanted to improve myself in some tangible way (can you tell TANGIBLE RESULTS had been drilled into my head for some time?!). My goal was to improve my Spanish language skills while traveling—ideally becoming bilingual—ahhh, lofty goals that one never quite achieves.

Learning the language would be critical to making my trip a success. I could be an ignorant tourist and get by with broken Spanglish, but that's not how I roll; correction, that's not how I wanted to roll anymore. Not to mention, I wanted to travel to remote destinations and I needed to be able to get from Point A to Point B, buy food, secure transport and lodging, ask for help if I needed it, and develop relationships.

Considering there is no better way to learn a language than to immerse yourself in it, I decided that I would take intensive courses and live with other students so we could practice together, ideally over a few glasses of the local malbec.

South America was also my destination of choice because my dollar would go further there than it would in many other places. Asia would have been a more economical choice, and a riveting choice at that, but I had already traveled to many places in Asia. I wanted to have new experiences and see new things while being able to communicate on some level. I had no chance with Mandarin (I am not proud to admit).

Finally, I had traveled to a few places in Central America before, enjoyed them, and thought, perhaps ignorantly, that South America would bear similarities while offering a brand-new experience at the same time. At the end of the day, it didn't take me long to decide on South America—perhaps an hour or so!

2

PREPARING FOR DEPARTURE

I began the preparations for my trip whilst still working. This was an intense time in my life—there were all kinds of arrangements to be made, from the travel plans themselves to farewell plans with friends and family. There was a seemingly endless amount of research to do, not only about different destinations, but also about what was required in order to visit those destinations (visas, vaccinations, etc.).

There were sacrifices to contend with—it would've been one thing to plan something like this with a limitless budget, but I had to deal with the reality of my financial situation. I wasn't flush with cash, but I intended to make this journey happen with some skilled budgeting and planning. I was a Finance Manager after all!

The planning process was exciting, filled with hopes, dreams, and a very special kind of anticipation. It was also laden with anxiety at times as I worked through all of the little details that needed to be taken care of in order to up-and-leave life as I knew it behind. I'd be remiss if I didn't mention that my job was demanding and still took up a majority of my time.

With all of this on my plate, I had to get organized and find a place to begin. For starters, I planned to read extensively about potential routes and destinations and I immediately purchased the Lonely Planet 'South America on a Shoestring' guide. This book was a great resource, but proved to be far too large and heavy to bring along with me on my travels. I basically read the whole thing, engrossing myself in it for a few hours every night before I went to bed, taking notes on important things in a small notebook that I planned to bring along with me.

Because I couldn't bring the large, heavy South America book with me, I traded it for an Argentina book before departure. This had several advantages: the Argentina-specific book would contain much more detail on the country I planned to visit first and it was much smaller and lighter! When I was ready, I would trade Argentina for the next country along my route so that I would only be carrying a guide for one country at a time (a strategy I learned from talking to other travelers).

A major factor that I needed to consider during my planning process was language. I would be traveling to countries where Spanish was the primary language, so I really needed to brush up on my Spanish language skills. I had some basic Spanish skills that I had acquired in high school, but this was not enough to get by.

I researched Spanish classes available in Buenos Aires and let's just say they weren't cheap. This was a bit worrying as I was going to be on a tight budget, but I knew the classes were essential. In my small, trusty notebook, I made yet another list that included the names of Spanish schools, their programs, prices, addresses, and reviews.

Another critical item on my planning list was to learn about entry requirements and any safety alerts for the countries I planned to visit. I started researching the necessary country basics on www.travel.state.gov, the 'official source' for things regarding visas and safety for Americans traveling abroad.

I kept notes on each country and started to make appointments to get required vaccinations. I determined whether or not I was permitted to enter certain countries based on my US citizenship. For those that I was allowed to enter, I applied for the visas I would need or noted exactly what was required for each if getting them in-country (things like local currency, vaccination forms, application forms, and identification).

I got a new passport photo and applied for a new passport because my research informed me that many countries require you to have a passport with at least six months remaining before expiration. My passport was close to expiration and nearly full, and I didn't want to take any chances (did I mention I was Type-A?!).

Over the span of a few months, I continued my research and showed up to the travel clinic for my vaccinations. I don't like to over-vaccinate and I'm also a huge wimp when it comes to needles, so this part was not fun for me.

Finally, as part of my planning process, I decided that I would write a blog in order to share my experiences with people back home and also to solicit recommendations and information from my social network. I worked on getting this up and running amidst the rest of my preparations.

Language lessons, visas, and vaccinations aside, I had to figure out when I would actually depart. There were a number of balls in the air: an apartment lease, a car to get rid of, money to save, and a job I had not yet quit. Timing was the next item on the agenda, and I needed to establish a timeline for departure to calm my nerves and give me a deadline to work toward.

3

TIMING

When I originally started thinking *seriously* about this trip (about nine months to a year prior to departure), I was promoted at work. Figures! Just when I think about removing myself from the rat race, I start winning it!

Many of those aware of my plans questioned whether I still intended to take the sabbatical considering my career was on the up-and-up, I was making more money, etc. I did not question whether or not I still wanted to take the trip, but questioned the timing. The promotion meant a higher bonus the following year, so if I could stick it out for a year, then I would get a nice chunk of change that could fund the trip.

However, I would then face the complication of having to find a place to live for over six months, as my apartment lease would end in the meantime. I spoke with my landlord to see if renting month-to-month was an option, but he required a full year commitment. Of course, the logistics were not the only issue—I would also have to continue working in my current environment, which was not exactly tempting (or was it too tempting?!).

Originally, I thought about staying with my newly married friends, Victoria and Kyle (my best friend and her husband), in their house in a suburb of Boston. I could offer to pay them a small sum for the use of their guest bedroom for a little while. However, six months is not exactly a little while, especially when you are encroaching on a married couple and their mean cat.

Moreover, I planned to sell my car and it would be tough to live in the burbs without wheels. I assessed the public transport options and the closest train station was over a mile away and the service was infrequent. This option just didn't seem feasible (FEASIBILITY—another business concept that was drilled into my head over the years).

I thought about putting all of my stuff in storage (and by storage, I mean above-mentioned extremely generous couples' basement, as I obviously couldn't be footing the bill for a real storage unit!) and renting a furnished room for a few months while I continued to save money and wait for that new and improved bonus check.

After reviewing these plans, potential snags, and what-ifs with good friends during many long car rides and long nights, an important reality brought itself to the forefront—I was not happy in my job. Why stay for another year when there is 'never a good time'? Don't get me wrong—I was very fortunate to have the job that I did. I took pride in my work and it stimulated my mind to a certain degree. In the early days at my company, I was happy there.

Time, perspective, and five different bosses later led me to the realization that I was not passionate enough about the role for it to make me truly content. While I enjoy business and finance and am a total math nerd deep inside, I realized I needed to apply my skills to something that I could get excited about. So, I planned to think about all of that and do some soul searching while on the sabbatical.

Ideally, I would eventually come home and become gain-fully employed with quickness in an industry I was wildly passionate about. That all said, I was far too financially unprepared to leave right away and had the apartment lease to worry about, so I needed to stick around for at least six months.

With all of these factors in mind, I thought about proposing a transition plan to my employer. Some friends advised me to keep quiet about my plans and just quit when I was ready to go. However, my team at work had recently undergone a great deal of change, and Boss Number Five was holding meetings with everyone on the team to evaluate their goals, strengths, weaknesses, etc.

I felt guilty going into a meeting like that pretending that I was gung-ho about my job and interested in progressing further. I wanted to help the team with the transition, and this would involve being honest so that they could find someone to replace me. The timing seemed right for me to propose a plan whereby I would stick around for a few months, train someone new, and continue to do my job (of course, with the benefit of getting paid all the while).

Proposing such a plan was very risky for me, as my new boss could have told to me leave immediately. I did lots of thinking about what that risk entailed (RISK ANALYSIS— need I say more?!). I also did lots of consulting with friends —friends who had wide-ranging opinions on the subject. One friend of mine who was a manager at a large company told me "If you came into my office and said you were quitting in a few months, I would tell you to pack your things and leave now."

Needless to say, I was uneasy, but I ultimately determined that I had enough leverage to go for it. The risk of the company wanting me to leave immediately was low (at least I thought so) and I was willing to accept the consequences if it went that way. If they told me to leave, I had a Plan B which was to look for temporary work until departure.

Fortunately, my proposal was accepted, and I truly believe it was a win/win for everyone. I was to remain gainfully employed until August of that year, and my team would benefit from the fruits of my labor for those next few months. The idea of an end date at work scared me. Things were getting real and all of the security that comes along with a regular paycheck was going out the window.

This brings me to the topic of my biggest fear throughout all of this—financial instability. Since I left home for college at the age of eighteen, I had supported myself (with a marginal loan for rent and incidentals from my parents during the college years). I was extremely independent, both emotionally and financially. In fact, after getting to know me, a coworker once said, "I felt sorry for you when you took this job. I didn't think you knew what you were getting yourself into. Then I realized that you are *fiercely* independent."

Regardless, I was afraid that I would have trouble finding a job when I returned home from my trip. I feared that I wouldn't find a job that paid as well as the job I had at the time. On the other hand, I feared that I would find a job that paid better, but didn't make me happy. The thoughts of returning home to unemployment, lack of financial stability, or a job I hated were my biggest fears—not getting kidnapped, killed in an earthquake, or attacked by a pack of piranhas.

I quieted my fears by assuring myself that I was a hard worker, I was smart, and I would land back on my feet. This self-assurance was not easy, but it was totally necessary in order to maintain sanity and move forward with my plans.

Once it was established that I would stop working in August and move out of my apartment on September 1st, I determined that I would most likely depart in September.

There was no point in sticking around while I wasn't making money when I could be living cheaper in the tropics. I planned to book the cheapest flight I could find in the September timeframe.

My first stop would be Buenos Aires. This would be the perfect jump-off point for my trip—it was a major city, so it was more likely that people would be able to speak English there, and this was important in the beginning. There were plenty of hostel options, the city had a variety of interesting neighborhoods, and I was sure to find quality Spanish classes there. Geographically, it was in a good position from which to embark on various routes to other interesting places.

One day during my lunch break at work, I booked a one-way ticket to Buenos Aires, which was a major milestone in my planning process and everything became very real. I felt a literal, physical rush throughout my body when I hit 'confirm' on the plane ticket purchase. I was set to depart on September 8th, 2014 at 7:30 PM. I would arrive in Buenos Aires on Tuesday, September 9th, at 10:00 AM. This was one of the fastest routes and would typically cost between $1,200.00 and $1,800.00.

Fortunately, I was able to apply some frequent flyer miles to the purchase, and I only ended up paying $250.00, which was fabulous considering my budget situation! Arriving in daylight hours was very appealing so that I could safely navigate to my hostel from the airport. Once I booked the ticket, it was time to get serious about my budget.

4

BUDGETING FOR THE BIG TRIP

When I told people about my plans, I heard a lot of "Wow, I wish I could do something like that!" This response frustrated me, as this opportunity was not handed to me on a silver platter. I remember thinking (but wisely keeping to myself), "If you wish you could do it, then do it," when people gave me that line.

Don't get me wrong, I understand that not everyone can just pick up and go, but most people can, even if they believe there are too many obstacles in their way. I was by no means wealthy in a monetary sense, and I was going to make this happen on a very tight budget with some serious planning and sacrificing. Anyone can do something like this if they are willing to make certain sacrifices.

It comes down to what you value—what you are willing to give up in order to get something else in return. While I absolutely realized that I may have been in a better position than many to do this, I also knew that folks did these kinds of things all the time with less. Entire families even did things like this!

Back to budgeting—my ability to become extremely frugal

14

during the time leading up to my trip amazed me (that and my prior tendency to drop large sums of cash on 'entertainment' on the weekends!). I started paying attention to every cent and equating every discretionary expense to what it could buy me on the road. I would think things like, "If I sacrificed going out for coffee three times a week for a month, I would have enough money for multiple nights of lodging."

I started to use coupons whenever I could, starting with a $20.00 REI coupon which I applied to the purchase of a small backpack and quick dry towel for my trip. The $20.00 I saved would afford me more than one night of lodging on the road. At one point leading up to my departure, I forgot my $7.00 worth of Stop & Shop coupons when I went grocery shopping, so the following week, I brought them to the customer service desk along with my receipt and got my $7.00 back. I felt like a crazy scratch ticket lady standing in line to do that, but hey, $7.00 could buy me dinner and a beer in most South American countries.

Acknowledging and embracing these tradeoffs was critical to making everyday sacrifices. My austerity plan was completely necessary to succeed in making my trip a reality. I had very little savings outside of my 401K plan and did not want to tap into that if I didn't absolutely need to. My friends made fun of me for my new frugal ways, but I didn't care.

In budgeting and saving money for a trip like this, there were various things that I needed to take into account (see Appendix for detailed tips on budgeting). I started by making a list of all of my expenses and categorizing them according to whether they were discretionary or not.

Next, I identified where I could cut costs from the discretionary expenses, which was fairly straightforward for me considering all of my discretionary spending went to what I broadly categorized as 'entertainment.' This included dining out, weekends away, golf tournaments, manicures, Uber and cab rides home after nights out on the town that had already broken the bank, etc.

All of these things made me happy, so it was difficult to think about sacrificing them. However, I realized that I didn't need to sacrifice everything—I just needed to be more selective about where I spent my money. Whenever I considered making a foolish expenditure, I would keep the end game in mind which was a very important strategy. I'd think to myself, "Would I rather have this immediate gratification, or would I rather bank this money to make my upcoming adventure even more awesome?"

This was kind of painful, but it was doable, and it was totally necessary as part of my austerity plan. I still took part in fun weekends away with friends, but I would buy food and booze for the house instead of going out and spending top dollar on these things. Little things like this saved me hundreds of dollars in no time!

Because food and drink were a big part of my life, I was able to cut costs in that arena quite easily. Some of my new strategies included bringing lunch to work, cooking at home, and going to friends' places for dinner. It became apparent very quickly that I was getting a lot more bang for my buck. A perfect example was the wine tradeoff—I could bring a bottle of wine to a friend's place for around $10.00, but I would spend more than that on just one glass if I went out for dinner!

Finding deals became a new strength of mine. Instead of spending $15.00 on a martini on a Friday night, I would go to places that served up $1.00 drafts. Eating at expensive restaurants became out of the question. Why would I need to do this when there were plenty of decent places with great food at lower prices?

A quick analysis of all of my memberships provided more

great cost cutting opportunities. I cancelled my gym membership and committed to working out outside and in my living room. Next on the chopping block were my cable, Netflix, and Spotify subscriptions.

I did not buy any new clothes for the season and instead mixed and matched what I already had. I only allowed myself to purchase key items that could be taken on the trip (i.e. quick dry, comfortable, versatile clothing).

My savings process involved not only cost cutting, but also revenue generating activities. I sold several items on eBay and craigslist which turned out to be easier than I thought it would be. Some examples of things I sold included:

- Old backpack for $25.00
- Pair of eyeglasses I would never wear again for $20.00
- One-piece ski suit for $35.00
- Air conditioner for $60.00
- Rollerblades for $50.00

These small sums really started to add up! I did not sell my furniture or TV, as I would need these things upon my return, so I stored them in my friend's basement. I got rid of my leased car by finding a dealer that would take it off my hands with no penalties.

I started to pay for absolutely everything with a credit card that earned points that could be used toward travel-related expenses. In order to avoid interest charges while still accruing points, I paid it off immediately every month. The plan was to use my accumulated points to pay for lodging, transport, etc. during my trip. I made sure I had a card with no foreign transaction fees so it could be used anywhere I traveled without additional charges.

When my apartment lease ended, I was able to crash with friends for the week before my departure date. I was and am very fortunate to have amazing people in my life that helped make my trip possible! I cannot express enough appreciation for the generosity that was shown to me by friends and family throughout my journey.

Although budgeting and saving are what I consider to be the *least* exciting parts of my trip, they were some of the *most* important. Anytime I made a sacrifice, I calculated how much I saved and transferred it to my travel savings account, even if it was literally $10.00. Once I got started, I found it addicting! Seeing my progress inspired me to challenge myself to save even more. I sacrificed bachelorette parties, weekends away on the beach, fun nights out on the town, etc. but it was all worth it when I was able to travel with the money I saved.

5
___

ONE MONTH TO DEPARTURE

The preparations necessary for this trip were extensive —much more so than I had imagined! One month prior to departure, I was in the thick of it. Obtaining the required and optional vaccinations (see Appendix for detail) were a high priority and before I could do that, I had to obtain my immunization history so that I knew what to get.

I visited a travel clinic to start the process of getting vaccinated, as this can take a while due to shots that are part of a series. Below is a list of the vaccinations I received and why:

- Yellow Fever: Imperative—a certification of this one was required to enter certain countries. I received a bright yellow, greeting card shaped certificate for this, which I put into my pile of 'very important things to pack.'
- Hepatitis A/B: Hepatitis B is a standard vaccination and most people have probably had it. However, Hepatitis A is considered 'travel-related.' Because I had not finished my Hepatitis B series, I was able to get a Hepatitis A/B combo series. This involved

three shots over a period of about one month, so I needed to plan accordingly to ensure I could complete these prior to departure. This was a highly recommended vaccine and one that I easily decided to get.

- Rabies: This was an optional three shot series. I had a tough time deciding on this one. My friend who had recently traveled long term in Asia did not get it and discouraged me a bit. There was also a chance that it wouldn't be covered by my insurance and would cost around $800.00. I considered the chances of getting attacked by a rabid dog or bat and unfortunately, deemed those chances to be pretty high.

Here's why—I was bitten by a wild monkey in Bali during a vacation once, which was terrifying (but apparently one of the most hilarious moments my friends ever witnessed). On the same trip, my friend was chased by a pack of stray dogs. Based on these experiences, I thought I better get the vaccine.

To make matters more confusing, though, I heard that if you were to get bitten by a rabid animal, the vaccine doesn't help you much and you still need to receive painful treatment. In the end, I believe I opted out of this one, but I honestly cannot recall for sure at the time of this writing!

- Typhoid: This can be given as a shot or an oral vaccine. It was highly recommended for most of the countries I was planning to visit, and I had heard a few stories about friends of friends getting typhoid. Not something I wanted to deal with on the road, so I opted for the oral vaccine (did I mention I was a wimp about needles?!).

The oral vaccine needed to be taken on an empty stomach in the morning for four consecutive days and you are not supposed to eat for an hour after taking it. As someone who eats breakfast the moment I wake up every day, I found it daunting to determine when I would be able to forgo an early breakfast for four days in a row, but I made it happen in the name of wanderlust!

In addition to the above vaccines, I also received medication for traveler's diarrhea, altitude sickness, and malaria to take along with me.

Figuring out my communication needs and methods was another priority. Initially, I did not plan to bring a phone with me on the trip and figured I could rely on my iPad and wireless internet access at hostels and cafés for communication.

Upon hearing the concerns of friends and family, I decided I would get a phone for emergencies. It would also be nice to have a phone for local use (meeting up with new friends, making transport arrangements, etc.). I did some research and found that you can buy SIM cards in the countries you visit and put them into an unlocked phone. With this in mind, I purchased a Samsung Galaxy from Amazon that would be compatible with T-mobile in the USA. I needed a phone before and after my trip as I would be turning in my work phone.

This first 'travel' phone I purchased needed to be returned because it was not actually unlocked as advertised. This was annoying, but I knew I couldn't expect everything to go smoothly with all of the preparations and I needed to roll with the punches! Finally, I obtained an unlocked Blu phone and got a pay-as-you-go plan to hold me over while I was still in the states. For $50.00 per month, I was able to get unlimited talk, text, and data.

In the end, I didn't even end up using local SIM cards to make phone calls. I learned that WhatsApp was the way to go to communicate with new travel buddies and that you should make all of your plans while you have access to WiFi. I used Facetime a few times to communicate with friends back home but aside from that, I kept in touch via email and social media.

So, my lesson learned here was that I didn't need to bother buying a special unlocked phone after all and using WiFi was the way to go. It's quite liberating to be unplugged for part of the day anyway!

In case of emergencies or sickness, I had to purchase insurance. I chose to get travel insurance through an organization called World Nomads based on recommendations from friends. I had reached the point in my preparations at which I could not be bothered to do additional research. Fortunately, I knew a few travelers who had used this insurance and had positive things to say about it.

To get me started, I purchased a four-month package at a total cost of $350.00. The insurance company allowed subscribers to add time to the policy at any point which was convenient considering the timeline of my trip was still up in the air. Travel insurance was a must and yes, I did use it for an infection I acquired toward the end of my trip (more on that later)!

As my preparations continued, I had to learn about the places that I would be traveling to—at least acquire a general understanding of the culture, weather, political situation, economy, etc. in each country. I started by checking out www. travel.state.gov, which provides great information on entry/exit requirements, embassies, and potential dangers.

For example, I learned that I would need to pay $160.00 for a reciprocity fee to enter Argentina, and that this needed to be paid online in advance of traveling. Furthermore, I needed to bring proof of payment with me. I learned that the 'street' or black-market exchange rate in Argentina was better than the bank rate. I also learned about the visa requirements and costs for a number of other countries.

As I mentioned before, I kept a small journal of critical information such as this. Note I said 'small' journal—I had to minimize bulk and weight wherever possible!

Researching weather patterns was also important and I investigated the weather in certain regions during certain times. This was a bit of a challenge, as I intended to wing it to a great extent, so I couldn't predict exactly where I would be and when. That said, I studied the general weather patterns during the general times I planned to be in certain places so that I knew what to pack for clothing. Packing for this trip was an undertaking in and of itself (an exciting one, though!) and I'll talk about this later.

My research was not yet complete! I researched Spanish classes, reading reviews and comparing prices and locations of various options. As I've mentioned, I planned to take intensive courses and there were many to choose from. Several people told me to ask around for recommendations once I had my feet on the ground, so I compiled a preliminary list of schools and addresses to aid in my detective work during my first week in Buenos Aires. The classes seemed to consistently start on Mondays and since I would arrive on a Tuesday, I would have plenty of time to check out the options before committing. I wanted to jump right in, but figured a week of exploring and getting my bearings would be useful.

As far as accommodations were concerned, I did some research on hostels in the city center of my first destination, Buenos Aires. I booked a hostel that was very centrally located for the first three nights of my trip. I intended to look at other hostels in person during my first week and decide if I would stay in the original one or move somewhere else.

In the past, I had found myself in plenty of situations where I wished that I had not booked the place I had in advance. I learned that pounding the pavement and looking for better options was a great alternative to booking everything ahead of time. You're probably thinking, 'Sounds risky!' if you're anything like me. Adopting this approach was tough for me as I was a *Big Huge Type-A Planner*, but as my trip unfolded, the value of pounding the pavement was really driven home for me.

That said, research on accommodation options was still very important. I was prudent enough to always have a backup plan, even looking into couchsurfing, which was all the rage at that time. At first, I shunned the concept, but after checking out the website, it seemed like a more viable option. There are references from other couchsurfers, and some people host hundreds of surfers and have well-established reputations.

Much of my preparation was focused on what to pack and bring with me. The mission was to bring as little as possible in order to lighten my load, but to have enough to live on for several months. I traveled with a large, typical 'backpacker's backpack' and a smaller, regular sized backpack as my luggage. As I laid out my gear on the bed of Victoria's guestroom, trying to pare things down, I knew the following items were must-haves for me (see Appendix for packing tips):

- Sport/waterproof/sweatproof sunscreen. Totally critical for a fair-skinned strawberry-blonde person! I knew I'd be able to acquire this along the way, but I most certainly needed a startup supply.
- Ibuprofen and prescription medications from the travel clinic.
- Strong deet bug spray.
- Quick dry towels (one normal size and one face cloth size).

- Travel bed sheet. I bought a travel 'cocoon' that folded down to nothing and could wrap up my whole body. Victoria made me demonstrate this as she observed me packing one day. We laughed uncontrollably as I laid on the bed wrapped up in my navy-blue cocoon.
- Ear plugs and eye mask.
- Bungee cord and carabineers. I knew these would come in handy for packing and any MacGyver-ing I may need to do.
- Small flashlight. I figured this would come in handy for walking in dark places (which I don't recommend doing alone!) or middle of the night trips to the bathroom.
- Hat. I brought a baseball cap for sun protection and to help me be more 'incognito' when I wanted to be. I thought a hat was also a nice way to represent where I was from and could serve as a conversation starter—Boston Red Sox, anyone?!
- Hiking boots.
- Flip flops. Not only for the beach, but also essential for hostel shower use!
- Sneakers. I knew I would be doing lots of walking.
- Scarf. A scarf can keep you warm, serve as a beach towel, or add some flare to a boring outfit, so this versatile item was a no-brainer for me.
- Versatile clothing. Unfortunately, I wouldn't be making any fashion statements on this trip (or perhaps I would be making ones I did not want to make!). My priority was quick dry clothing that was neutral or dark in color and that could be layered, mixed, and matched. The layering part would come in handy for various climates.

I packed a lightweight full-zip North Face fleece, a Helly Hansen rain coat, lightweight hiking pants that could be zipped off into shorts, a few breezy dresses, one pair of jeans, and some T-shirts. One of the key items I packed was a long sweater with an Aztec-like pattern that could be dressed up or down. My friends fondly referred to it as 'the South America sweater' considering how much wear it got! Also, they will never let me live down the pants that zipped off into shorts!

- Toiletries. Simple makeup was a must have for me. While I vowed to be a low maintenance traveler, I knew I would still like to get dolled up occasionally, so I packed minimal makeup. I also packed travel size shampoo, conditioner, soap, and toothpaste, but only one set of this stuff as I knew these items could be purchased along the way and I didn't want to add unnecessary weight. Since I heard that tampons could be hard to come by in certain countries, I packed a decent supply of compact-size tampons.
- Local currency. I got some local currency for my first country in advance from my bank so that I had something to hit the ground running with. I got approximately $100.00 USD worth as I didn't want to get so much that I would be in a bad place if I was robbed, but I also wanted enough for a meal, a taxi, and a night of lodging while I figured out the local cash situation.
- Emergency stash of US dollars. I wanted to have this so that I could get that black-market exchange rate on the street where applicable (and just because)! At the time, USD were very highly valued and would give me some bargaining power.

Again, I didn't want to bring too much because getting robbed is a real possibility! I carried around $250.00 with me in a money belt to start.

- Money belt. I felt a little ridiculous wearing this, but I had read that it is a prudent safety measure. A money belt is basically a flat pouch of sorts that can be strapped around your body (under your clothes) to hold your valuables in case your backpack and/or purse is stolen.

- Inflatable pillow. I knew I would be taking various modes of transportation and I wanted to be as comfortable as possible. Instead of a classic airport neck pillow, I bought one that you can blow up and deflate as needed. When deflated, it was totally flat, which was great for packing.

- Travel documents. My passport was probably the number one item on the packing list! I also brought copies of my passport so that I could leave my actual passport locked up while I was out and about in different places. I left additional copies with friends and family at home as well. Finally, I brought my yellow fever vaccination card, immunization history report, travel insurance confirmation, and some spare passport photos for use in obtaining visas.

As my departure date neared, I changed my address and forwarded my mail to my mother. I also gave her a checkbook of mine, as I trusted her to manage any bills that may have come along. Considering many international ATMs will not accept a long pin number (I learned this the hard way), I changed my ATM pin to four digits. Finally, I notified my bank and credit card companies of my travel plans so my cards wouldn't get shut off.

Intentionally, I avoided planning too much of the actual trip. As I mentioned, I booked three nights in a hostel for the very beginning so that I would have a destination upon arrival. My first 'home' was called Hostel Estoril and was located in downtown Buenos Aires, Argentina.

When determining where to stay, I read reviews on Tripadvisor and other sites and assessed the location. I only booked a few nights because I wanted the option to move if I didn't like the hostel and/or I saw something more desirable. I figured that I would probably stay in Buenos Aires for at least a few weeks and evaluate my next significant move after getting some of those Spanish classes under my belt.

While I didn't have a detailed itinerary for my trip, I had an idea of what I wanted to do. At a very high level, I had some 'definites' on my route, a mishmash of cities, regions, and countries: Buenos Aires, Patagonia, Mendoza, Chile, Bolivia, and Peru. If I wound up with any money left after hitting these places, I wanted to visit Colombia, Ecuador, and more!

Finally, it was time to pack up my apartment. Because the duration of my trip was undefined, I planned to move out of my apartment as opposed to paying rent for a place I would not be living in for months. I arranged to rent a U-Haul truck for the big move, but I eased the burden by moving a carload of stuff per week to my friend's place in advance of the final move. This worked out very well, as I got something productive done each week and got to spend some time with my friends. We would usually get a beach day and dinner in on the days I moved things as we soaked up the end of summer together.

6

SACRIFICING THE AMENITIES OF HOME

I accepted and embraced the fact that my lifestyle was going to change dramatically on September 9th, 2014 at 10:00 AM when I stepped off the plane in Buenos Aires. That said, there were some amenities of home that I had to get used to going without.

The good news was that I had already started to become accustomed to living out of a bag before the trip, considering I moved out of my apartment a week or so in advance. However, prior to my trip, I still had a home base (my friends' house) and I would no longer have that once I was on the road.

I am a little embarrassed to admit that I was apprehensive about sacrificing my daily makeup routine. During the few years preceding my travels, I had been investing in nicer products and makeup like a true diva. I developed a preference for MAC and Bare Minerals products, and I knew I was more beautiful because of it (Dear Marketing Departments, if you read this and would like to send me free makeup, I will gladly continue to discuss the merits of your products).

In my new life, I would not only have insufficient funds

for expensive makeup, but I would also not be able to wear much makeup. First off, I knew it would just sweat right off of my face anyway in some of my destinations and secondly, I certainly did not want to look too high maintenance for the environments I would be in. This saddened me, as I was not one for the au natural look at that point in my life.

While I wasn't a fresh-faced twenty-something back-packer, I accepted that I would have to whittle down my routine and settle for simple products that I could find in the local farmacia (which I knew would probably be appallingly priced imports). I was certain that I would not be visiting any department store counters in my near future. Looking on the bright side, I was confident that I would stop taking small luxuries for granted and perhaps even embrace my natural beauty!

Along similar lines, I would be forgoing the benefits of a blow dryer and hair straightener. These are two items that most girls take for granted and don't leave home without when traveling even for a long weekend. I would have to succumb to the ginger lion's mane that is my untamed hair. Interestingly enough, I hardly ever blew my hair dry or straightened it again after my travels! And my makeup routine has remained low maintenance even years after my trip!

Continuing on the subject of toiletries and sacrifices, my thoughts turned to toilet paper and how I preferred my TP on the thicker, softer side. But who was I kidding? In a few short weeks, I'd be lucky if I remembered to steal some napkins at lunch to use in the sketchy bathrooms I would encounter! Again, a small luxury that I was more than willing to go without.

My wardrobe would be yet another loss. There would no longer be a variety of clothes, or even clean clothes for that matter, in my life for a while. I would look like a traveling hippie with my uniform of quick dry hiking pants or jeans and neutral-colored polyester shirt. I planned to treat myself to a dress or other clothing necessity at the local market here and there, but a wide-ranging wardrobe doesn't fit into a backpack, so I would have to make do.

Speaking of that backpack, that would become my new home base. I would no longer have an apartment to call my own and in which to spread out my things as I pleased on multiple surfaces.

Ahhhh, my bed. My new plush, outrageously comfortable queen-sized bed with soft, clean sheets and multiple pillows. Goodbye my loooove. Hello top bunk with old dirty mattress, one lifeless pillow, and traveling cocoon bedsheet.

Switching gears to technology, my iPhone was a sacrifice (which in hindsight, I realized I didn't have to make). I started using a Blu brand phone, as it was compatible with the cell frequencies and SIM cards in South America. The phone adjustment was more difficult than I anticipated. It took me a while to get used to the different functionality. Unfortunately, the camera was also terrible on the Blu phone and I wouldn't be able to count on it for any quality pictures. For photo-taking, I brought my digital camera (by the time you are reading this, digital cameras will be a relic of the past, I'm sure!).

Giving up my car was easier said than done, purely due to the logistics. At the time, I was leasing a Honda CRV and I tried to get out of the lease a few months prior to the trip. However, I was told I had negative equity in the car and would have to pay $1,500.00 to get out of it. I decided against that, as I would pay about that in car payments anyway if I held it until lease maturity and would have the added convenience of coming back to a car.

That said, I decided I would give it another go when I came closer to departure. Besides, I needed my car for my few weeks of 'funemployment,' moving, and errand running leading up to the trip. Closer to my departure date, I brought the car to a different dealer and had them appraise it to see if I could get out of the lease early. It was a last-ditch effort so that I wouldn't have to carry the anxiety of paying for a car that I wasn't driving for months.

Success! They agreed to pay off the car and take it off my hands then and there. I was shocked since I had been putting a lot of miles on it during my funemployment stint, but I took the license plates, threw them in my beach bag, and had Victoria pick me up at the dealer!

The ability to spend money freely was another big sacrifice for me. I was fortunate enough to have reached a point in my career where I had discretionary income to spend on things I wanted, not just things I needed. Now, each future purchase would make me anxious considering I would not be employed during my travels, and all funds would be coming out of my savings account.

The anxiety surrounding money started even before I departed. I was finding it difficult to keep my spending on food down, as I was staying at different places and doing lots of running around, which contributed to a lot of eating on the go. All of the running around had also caused me to give up certain routines—not only when it came to eating, but also when it came to working out and other general daily patterns. I tried to squeeze in workouts and eat healthy, but that is definitely not as easy when you are not living at your home with your standard routines in place (excuses, excuses!).

Finally, I had to give up my close support network (or at least my proximity to it). My friend Victoria's home was an amazing transition spot for me—I had my own space, a place to shower and do laundry, and friends around to provide advice and moral support when I needed it. There were always plenty of friends around who would get me laughing when I was down about leaving my apartment of five years, or provide input on whether I should pack the lightweight fleece, the Under Armor base layer, or both.

While all of the above sounds quite high maintenance, I wanted to be real about what you give up when you leave the comforts of home. Obviously, I was willing to make the sacrifices in order to travel long term and experience the world. I had a very modest upbringing, did not feel entitled to anything, and was very willing and able to go without. In fact, I thought it would be fun (right?!?!).

7

ONE HOUR UNTIL LIFTOFF

W hen departure day finally arrived, I found myself sitting in Logan Airport heavily buzzed after sharing a bottle of farewell bubbly with Victoria, reflecting on the prior three weeks of unemployment, freedom, fun, apprehension, and preparation.

The following phrases kept popping into my thoughts and I giggled to myself:

Are you going ALONE?!?!?!
Aren't you SCARED?!?!?!
Won't you be LONELY?!?!?!
Wow, that takes BALLS!

The few weeks leading up to my trip were filled with firsts, lasts, laughter, and tears. On my last day of work, I left the office at noon—there was nothing productive I was going to accomplish on that last day and I was getting sad about leaving certain people. My colleagues had already thrown me two parties and I had a desk full of parting gifts to remind me of my impending departure.

It was very surreal as I walked out of the revolving door of my fancy downtown office for the last time—bittersweet indeed.

Sitting on a bench in Boston's Greenway, I read the cards that my colleagues had written me and tried to fight back tears unsuccessfully as I waited for my soon-to-be-temporary-roomie/best pal to pick me up for a much-needed champagne-fueled lunch.

My first week off was occupied with packing, taking trips to goodwill to donate items I no longer needed, shopping for items I did need, and moving. The move out of my apartment went smoothly thanks to my little brother, his friend, and my new roomies. We had pizza and beer when it was finished as you do on any typical moving day.

The feeling of nostalgia as I left my apartment for the last time was a lot stronger than I had anticipated. As I took one last look around at the empty rooms, I shed a few tears—I had lived in the place for five very formative years (ages twenty-eight through thirty-two) and there were a lot of memories within those walls. It was a very strange feeling closing the door behind me for the last time (or what I thought was the last time).

Of course, I left something important behind—the refrigerated typhoid vaccine I needed to take—so I had to torture myself with another sad walkthrough when I went back for it. Because I forgot the vaccine and had my mind in a million different places, I didn't get the timing of the dosage quite right but I hoped for the best!

The final two weeks preceding departure were spent catching up with family and good friends. I fondly reminisced on the things we did. I spent quality time with my Mom—we took a sunset harbor cruise and spent a night camping (well, I guess you could call it glamping . . . we had a cabin in the woods).

As you can imagine, my mother was not exactly thrilled about the prospect of her daughter embarking on a journey such as this. Thankfully, she was very supportive. I'm sure she realized she wouldn't change my mind, so why bother trying. As any mother would, she pleaded with me to be careful, stay in touch as much as possible, and not walk down dark alleys alone. I assured her that this trip was something I *really* wanted to do, so if God forbid anything happened to me, just know that I died happy. I'm sure that was really encouraging!

My goodbyes carried on with a quintessential New England theme as I spent some time in Cape Cod with friends, relaxing and biking along the Cape Cod Canal and Rail Trail. Continuing to soak up the summer on the coast, I spent a day boating and hanging out on Rainsford Island, a favorite Boston Harbor Island of mine, and spent another day at Duxbury Beach. On the beach, Victoria and I practiced our Spanish skills with my handy book over a few cocktails.

There were BBQs, golf outings, and lunches at favorite places. The final hurrah was an amazing sendoff party with lots of great friends, followed by a day of recovery that involved watching Sunday football, complete with a delicious and highly satisfying last supper of homemade chili and nachos. Between all of these social engagements, I hustled to get last minute items for my trip.

As I got dressed and put the last items into my bag on departure day, I had butterflies in my stomach as reality set in. Victoria drove me to the airport and we got on the road early to avoid Boston traffic and ensure we had enough time to stop at the airport Hyatt for a farewell bottle of bubby with a view (which has now become a tradition for us).

We both shed a few tears on the ride to the airport as Victoria played an excruciatingly appropriate soundtrack including Kenny Chesney's 'She's from Boston.' I made sure to properly freak her out by informing her about my different accounts and asking her to ensure that if I never returned, the little money I had was to go to my mother.

Those few weeks made me realize how absolutely amazing my family and friends are. I was (and am) so grateful for all of the generosity that was shown to me, for every offer to hop on a plane to save me if necessary, for every meaningful card and gift, for every complimentary meal and cocktail, for every travel tip, etc. There is far too much to note! I was especially grateful to Victoria and Kyle for housing me and my belongings, and putting up with my idiosyncrasies as I imposed upon them for a few weeks.

I was very excited to begin the next chapter in my life, so off I went!

8

THE INITIAL JOURNEY

I wish I could say the initial journey was smooth, but these things never are! On a positive note, I began my journey with empty seats next to me on both legs of the trip to Buenos Aires. This was awesome, as I was able to stretch out and relax. However, upon boarding the overnight leg from Miami, the auxiliary power on the plane was not working. This meant no air conditioning until the engines were started —no biggie, right? Well, I didn't think so either until we lost *all* power and sat at the gate for two hours in a complete sweat pit. The power kept flickering on and off and people would clap and groan respectively.

I kept wondering when I would get my dinner and vino so I could take my Advil PM and put myself down for the redeye flight per my original plan. Side note—NEVER have an 'original plan' that you are stuck on or you will be regularly and sorely disappointed!

A few hours after boarding in Miami, we finally departed and a smooth flight ensued. I had pre-booked a shuttle from the airport to downtown Buenos Aires, as my research had shown that shuttles were much cheaper than taxi rides, and there's nothing wrong with safety in numbers!

Due to the flight delay and lack of clarity on the meeting point for the shuttle, I missed the 12:00 PM departure by the skin of my teeth. I killed two hours at the airport McDonald's waiting for the next shuttle, as I refused to spend cash on cab fare on Day One, and particularly in this situation. I knew I would encounter situations where I would be willing to pay for convenience but I also knew I needed to deal with minor inconveniences to save a few bucks when possible.

The airport scene in Buenos Aires was reminiscent of many I had experienced in Asia. Total 'cluster F' with people holding signs bearing names of travelers, yelling out names, soliciting, etc. Within five minutes of walking through the Arrivals door, an American guy approached me to ask what flight I was on because he was waiting for somebody. Gee, I wonder what made me stick out of the crowd?! Was it the ginger hair or the double backpacks?

Anyway, we got to chatting since I couldn't find my shuttle man, and of course Question Number Two from said American stranger was "Did you come here alone?" I had done some reading on how to deal with these situations and even though this guy was a seemingly very normal, non-threatening Texan, I said I was meeting people.

A few minutes later, one of the countless policemen milling around gave me a flyer warning against accepting rides from unestablished companies. Nice little safety assurance there, but I was obviously given the flyer because I was a foreign solo woman and it was not hard to notice that pretty quickly.

So, I debated putting on my 'wedding ring.' I read that wearing a band to appear married can discourage some unwanted advances, and of course, being totally Type-A, I was in possession of such a band. I chose to bring a simple, faux gold band that had come as part of a set of costume jewelry that I had purchased long ago. While the possession of the band gave me a sense of security, I decided not to put it on at that particular point—I was feeling very safe so far, but I had a feeling it was going to come in handy.

As I mentioned, I killed the time between shuttles at the airport McDonald's. While I rested, I drank a soda to keep me awake until the next shuttle came. To fill the time, I wrote a blog entry to update my people back home on my safe arrival. I thought about how it would be challenging to keep up with the blog once I was having a kick ass time and not sitting at an airport McDonald's.

My blog was called 'Ginger Adventures' and I was anxious to get the real adventure started. My friend Landon nick-named me 'Ginger Danger' and thereafter commented, 'Ginger. Danger.' on all of my social media posts. The nickname has stuck to this day!

I couldn't wait to get out of the airport and have some fun. There was something nagging at me, though—I was having trouble deciphering whether the immigration officer wrote '20' or '90' days on my passport. The officers can use their discretion, which is why I was paranoid that it said '20.' However, the official limit was 90. If it indeed said 20, I would have some imminent planning to do, as I would need to go over to Chile earlier than intended in order to come back into Argentina for a fresh stamp. Not exactly ideal, as it would make me feel a bit rushed but I knew I would work it out either way.

Considering my usual Type-A personality, I was surpris-ingly relaxed and flexible about the travel snafus that had arisen thus far (I knew my friends would be proud)!

9

THE FIRST FEW DAYS: BUENOS AIRES

After being stuck in the Buenos Aires airport for hours due to the flight delay and missing the noon shuttle, I finally arrived at my hostel around 4:00 PM. Initially, I wasn't sure I was in the right place, as the signage outside was not obvious. My heart raced a bit as I thought, "Am I in the right location? Is someone going to be here to check me in? What if it's closed and locked?"

After noticing a small sign indicating the hostel was on the first floor, I searched around the 'first floor' as I knew it, which is the ground floor in American terms. Because I couldn't find anything that resembled a hostel entrance, I walked up a fairly grand, twisting staircase to investigate further. Lo and behold, there was the entrance (and I soon learned that first floor in Latin American terms equals second floor in USA terms).

The door was locked so I rang the bell and was greeted by a friendly man, who I later learned was the owner. After a quick check-in process, I was shown to my room, which ended up being an all-girls room despite the fact that I had booked the mixed dorm (the place was overbooked and the only availability was in the all-girls room).

Originally, I had booked the mixed dorm simply because of the cheaper rate, but after being in the hostel for about fifteen minutes, I realized I was lucky to have been moved to all-girls. One glimpse into the boys' room cemented the fact that a few extra bucks a night for all-girls would be factored into my budget going forward.

Step One was to lock up my valuables and take a stroll around to familiarize myself with the layout of the place. I secured a small locker since the girls in the room had already claimed the larger, better ones. The small one was sufficient to lock up my valuables, however. I was assigned to a bottom bunk in the six-bed dorm room. Three sets of wood-framed bunkbeds occupied most of the purple-walled room. A large, beautiful arched Victorian window took up most of one wall, allowing light and air to spill into the room. Used bath towels hung from the posts on the bunkbeds and an empty beer bottle sat atop one of the lockers.

The hostel itself occupied two floors (first and sixth, not to be confused with second and seventh!), and my room was on the sixth floor, which had two nice terraces where people could sit outside to eat and hang out. From the top terrace, there was a view of the busy thoroughfare below, the surrounding cityscape, and the questionable electric wiring that hung throughout the city. The sixth floor also had an indoor common area that was furnished with a few couches, a TV, and several bookshelves from which guests could borrow or trade travel guides or novels.

The first floor had a much nicer and bigger common area, a large kitchen, and an interior courtyard. You could buy beer, water, and soda from the front desk staff or bartender if one was on duty. The front desk staff and bartenders were gener-ally hostel guests who worked in exchange for free or discounted accommodation. I wasn't yet sure if you could buy food at the hostel, but I knew breakfast was included.

That first evening, I was pretty exhausted from my travels, so I had a slice of pizza for dinner from a place directly next door to the hostel. Someone recommended it to me and considering its proximity and my fatigue, it was a no brainer. I had pizza from there yet again for lunch the following day as I slowly came out of my traveling fog. What I didn't realize yet was that Buenos Aires has a significant Italian influence, and thanks to that, the pizza was great.

I beat myself up a bit for how unhealthy I was eating, but I figured it was a transition period, and I would find the right places soon enough.

It was weird sleeping in the dorm room the first night and I wondered about the norms surrounding lights and noise, etc. My roommates were generally very respectful, and even when coming in at all hours of the night, they were quiet (or at least they thought they were!). Wearing ear plugs and an eye mask was totally necessary—wearing these felt very foreign to me at first, but I got used to them quickly and soon couldn't live without them.

One of my primary tasks was to find a Spanish school, so on my first full day in Buenos Aires, I ventured out to visit three schools within walking distance of my hostel. The walk to the first school took me across the busiest boulevard in the world, a ten-lane thoroughfare that was impossible to cross in one go. As I walked along, I took in my new surroundings.

The city had a very European feel—old buildings complete with ornate domes, arched windows, and wrought iron balconies dominated the cityscape. Flawlessly painted graffiti decorated the walls of several edifices. The windows of storefronts were filled with colorful wares like socks, shoes, purses, etc. Signs advertising restaurant promotions peppered the sidewalks.

Enrique Iglesias's hit, Bailando, blasted from cars and restaurants, mixed with the background sounds of honking and busy traffic that you would find in any bustling metropolis.

The first school I visited was the least expensive and I really liked it so I thought I would probably opt for that one. However, I wanted to give myself one more day to explore another neighborhood before committing. An American girl at my hostel offered to bring me to her school to check it out, so I thought about doing that, but it was kind of out of the way and I wanted something convenient.

I couldn't wait to start school, as I felt timid about speaking Spanish in fast-paced restaurant situations and asking questions in stores, etc. I wanted to learn more and boost my confidence ASAP.

During the day's travels on Day One, I stopped into a hostel that I recognized as a 'top choice' from my guidebook. I wanted to execute some due diligence and ensure that I wasn't missing out on any better options. It turns out that I did not like the place as much as the one I was already checked into. I thought I would likely extend my stay at my original hostel—I really liked the vibe and accommodations.

Continuing along my travels during Day One, I purchased a SIM card for my phone at a kiosko (a little market/convenience store that can be found everywhere around Buenos Aires). The card was not working properly at first, and the guys working at the store helped me figure it out as we communicated in broken Spanish and English (a.k.a. Spanglish). They were extremely helpful, which I soon realized was the norm. The Argentinian people were proving to be very friendly and welcoming so far.

While I saw a few sights on Day One, I was saving the more in-depth sightseeing for once I was situated. Type-A Kerie needed to get settled into school and a routine of some sort as the first order of business. Even though I wasn't trying, I did some accidental sightseeing while running my errands, stumbling across several interesting buildings and monuments along my way. 'Don't Cry For Me Argentina' played on repeat in my head all day, which I attributed to the fact that there was a huge painting of Eva Peron on the side of a building on my new block!

The next day, I was ready to tackle some more items on my to-do list. After cleaning myself up enough to be presentable (so long, rolling out of bed with messy hair and PJs for brekkie in private), I ventured to the breakfast area on the sixth floor.

Breakfast was very basic and consisted of a basket of white breads set on each communal table along with tubs of jam, dulce de leche, and butter. When I say tubs, I'm talking half gallon containers that have been open for God-knows-how-long and touched by God-knows-how-many used utensils! There were corn flakes and coffee to be had as well. If you woke up early enough, there were delicious croissants with a honey glaze called medialunas, but these went fast! All very healthy stuff—NOT!

As I sat down to my first breakfast, an Australian guy sitting at the same table offered me some cereal and bananas that he had purchased on his own. It was a very nice gesture and I felt happy to be meeting friendly people right off the bat. I stuck with two pieces of bread with jam, butter, and dulce de leche but figured I would test out the first-floor breakfast the next day (they supposedly served eggs—luxury!). I also made a mental note to buy some emergency staples.

During my travels over the next few days, I bought some

yogurt, wrote my name on it with a Sharpie, and put it in the very full communal fridge.

Meeting people proved to be very easy, and I met some great folks at the hostel in no time. Hostel life centers around community which is one of the main reasons I had chosen this type of accommodation. While hanging out in the common areas, I quickly met people from all over the world —an American girl, an English girl, two Canadian guys, a French guy, a German guy, an Ecuadorian guy, a South Korean girl, a Thai guy, and others. It was challenging to keep the names and stories of these people straight, which I was sure would become a trend. Sitting in the common areas, I got to chatting with people about potential day trips, weekend trips, and longer-term itineraries.

Roommates were another source of potential friends and acquaintances. One of my roommates, Scarlett, a pretty fair-haired Brazilian girl, sold me an adapter for fifteen pesos when I inquired about where I could buy one. At the prevailing street rate, that was equivalent to about one US dollar. Sweet deal, and I even got to test the product before committing.

Believe it or not, another roommate (the girl in the bed right next to me) was a Bostonian. She was younger than me but very friendly, and as we got to chatting, she invited me to a music show on the following Friday night. My other roommates were Australian and Belgian women, which I gleaned from the usual, "Hello, I'm so-and-so, where are you from?" conversation. Three of the girls in my room were staying there for free in exchange for working reception and bar. I planned to investigate this possibility for myself.

Everyone was very helpful and quick to offer tips to the new traveler on the scene. Some especially valuable tips from the girls in my room included which shower was the best and where to eat.

In addition to securing schooling, one of my priorities during the first week of the trip was to exchange some money. My roommate Jan, the Australian woman, offered to go with me when she overheard me talking to someone else about the topic. It was another kind gesture and I felt good about the way people were looking after one another.

With regards to the exchange rate, you could get fifteen pesos per one US dollar on the street, twelve pesos per dollar in the hostel, and eight pesos per dollar at banks. Apparently, a popular option was to take the ferry across the Rio de la Plata to Uruguay to get USD (you couldn't get USD in Argentina at the time) and bring them back to exchange on the street in Buenos Aires. I figured I would get some more information on that and find some partners in crime that wanted to spend a weekend in Colonia, Uruguay sightseeing and ATM-hitting.

As I went about those initial days in Buenos Aires, I quickly learned the prices of key items in my everyday life. Below is a list that will give you an idea of the prices of things in 2014 once the 'blue dollar' (unofficial black market) exchange rate was taken into account. I was struck by the relative low cost of certain things and high cost of others.

Typical Prices in USD—Buenos Aires 2014:

- One-liter bottle of water: $1.00 - $1.50
- Coffee + three medialunas (croissants) or tostados (ham and cheese sandwiches) + orange juice: $3.00
- Empanada: $0.80
- Quality salad at a lovely takeout place: $2.00
- Steak dinner with wine, starters, and sides: $15.00
- One night of accommodation in a hostel dorm room: $10.00 - $18.00
- 17-hour bus ride: $70.00

- New Nike sneakers: $55.00
- One intercity bus or subway ride: $0.25
- Boat tour of canals in a neighboring city (Tigre): $5.00
- Pack of cigarettes: $1.25
- Bottle of wine from supermarket: $2.00
- Most expensive museum ticket: $3.50
- Ticket to the movies: $0.50

The hostel held a variety of social events, and I was looking forward to my first weekly asado (BBQ), where everyone would get together for a big meal on the terrace. I was super excited because I really liked the people whom I had briefly met thus far and it would be a great opportunity to get to know them better. Social opportunities were not difficult to come by at the hostel, and I spent the majority of those first few evenings on the terrace having a few beers with other travelers, chatting about our respective journeys, and sharing advice.

While the first few days of the trip went swimmingly by any standards, there were small challenges that had to be dealt with. One of my initial trials involved constantly digging through my bags for things I needed and determining where to put things. Without the luxuries of a dresser, a closet, or any kind of personal surface area upon which to place things, it was tough to stay organized—however, I could see that I would become more efficient at living out of my backpack as time passed.

Another small challenge was getting used to sharing bathrooms with a myriad of other folks—the bathrooms were obviously not Ritz quality, but they were sufficient. Interestingly enough, bidets were a common feature in the bathrooms around town (once, I had to use one to wash my feet off after stepping in a disgusting puddle!). Seeing other peoples' hair on the shower walls or in the drain was disconcerting, but I had mentally prepared for these types of things. While I would occasionally get grossed out, it was a small price to pay for the adventure I was on.

Overall, I was enamored so far! Buenos Aires is a beautiful city bustling with life and culture, set among a stunning architectural backdrop. The weather was glorious in September—blue skies and temperatures in the sixties. I was feeling good about everything (albeit tired) and had no regrets about my decision to take the journey.

10

BUENOS AIRES CONTINUED...

Week One in Buenos Aires was a real whirlwind and feast for the senses—I quickly lost track of time and found it arduous to keep up with my blog. My life was quite busy with school, new friends, and being a tourist.

On one of my first nights in town, I was invited to dinner at a parilla (typical Argentinian steak house) with seven fellow travelers from the hostel. It was an interesting, eclectic, and inspiring crew to say the least. We swapped stories and tips over a decadent dinner of empanadas, beef, potatoes, and lots of red wine. Before dinner, we had a few drinks at a Che Guevara-themed bar—this place was really something, decorated from top to bottom in Che-themed swag. I made a note to self to learn more about this man and why he was so revered.

After dinner, our crew returned to the hostel, where hilarity ensued as we drank beer out of coffee mugs, watched Shakira videos, and danced on the sixth-floor terrace. There, I met Luca, an amazingly flamboyant Venezuelan gay man, who liked to go by 'Posh Spice' and gave me the moniker 'Ginger Spice.' Luca's personality was larger than life and he cracked me up with his mannerisms and the crazy things he said while pretending to be Victoria Beckham.

The social scene continued to flourish as Week One continued on. The hostel's weekly asado took place on my first Saturday night, which was a big party that entailed lots of eating, socializing, and serious laughs. The evening started with a dinner of endless grilled meats and concluded on the roof terrace with a game of flip cup with a bunch of Irish newcomers.

At one point during the evening, a Chilean guy told me he heard that if you try to kiss a Boston girl, she will do the 'cobra,' which means quickly lean away. The perceptions people had of Americans, and Bostonians for that matter, were too funny. While I laughed, I also thought to myself, "Yeah, buddy, I'll show you the cobra for real if you try to make a move!"

In addition to partying with my newfound pals, I tried to get some of the major sights in during Week One. The day after the hostel's asado, I visited Recoleta cemetery (where Eva Peron, 'Evita,' is buried) with a Finnish girl I met at dinner, her Finnish friend, and a local couple that they knew. It was nice to have locals with us—they shared great information and helped us navigate our way around the city. We picked up delicious sandwiches in a lovely little sandwich shop that I never would've discovered on my own, and had lunch in a pretty, green park. We did lots of walking around the city that day, so I took a siesta afterwards (the night before eventually caught up with me)!

Another day during my first week, a group of folks from the hostel invited me to join them on a bike ride. We took free city bikes to Puerto Madero, a nature reserve by the water. There, we saw some interesting bird life and I caught my first glimpse of the Rio de la Plata, the delta between Argentina and Uruguay.

As if the week couldn't get more action-packed, I was invited to cook some dinner in the hostel with a group of others on yet another night. Of course, I accepted. Dinner hour in Latin America is much later than I was accustomed to, so I had to get used to eating dinner at 10:00 PM.

I also had to become accustomed to the 'mañana' mode of operation—putting things off that don't need to be done today—and a much slower pace overall. For example, if someone said they were going to do something in thirty minutes, that typically meant at least an hour. Experiencing this slower pace was very good for my overly Type-A personality!

But back to dinner . . . on that particular night, four of us gathered and roasted a variety of meats and vegetables, served with mashed cauliflower and some nice local malbec. I was impressed with how my new friends could whip up a nice meal out of seemingly nothing! After dinner, I did what became my normal routine—had drinks on the terrace with people from all around the world speaking Spanglish. This was one of my favorite things to do! It was such a great opportunity to be able to sit among a group of people that speak many different languages and learn from them.

We would all sit in a circle, have drinks, share stories, and laugh. One of the guys, Victor (pronounced 'Wictor' by my new German friend Frederik, which I loved), gave me his remaining marijuana after we smoked a friendly joint or two on the rooftop. Victor was returning to France and wouldn't be able to bring it with him.

While I was getting by, I felt very ignorant with regards to my language skills. I really hoped the classes would help, signing up and taking the 'level test' during Week One. I would start school on Monday of Week Two and would be in a class with a few others at a similar Spanish level. My class would run from 10:00 AM - 2:00 PM every weekday.

I was chomping at the bit to start so I could improve my speaking skills. It is sad that we don't learn another language while we are young in America. Pretty much everywhere else in the world, the people learn at least one more language at a young age. I thought that if I ever had a child, I would make sure they learned different languages as soon as they could speak!

As for practical matters during my first week away, my bungee cord came in handy right off the bat. I had packed a bungee cord with duct tape wrapped around it in case I needed either of these items for anything. One night, I noticed Scarlett struggling with the window in our 'bedroom.' The window would not stay closed on its own and it was cold outside, so I volunteered my bungee cord and we bungeed the window closed. Successful MacGyver mission!

While I was adapting to hostel life quite nicely, it of course had its ups and downs. One of the downsides involved sniffing my clothes on a regular basis to see if they were suitable for additional wears. In terms of upsides, I snagged the big locker near my bed when someone checked out, and I was getting my bathroom routine down (although I still always managed to forget something).

It was challenging to share a room with five others because you needed to be quiet when people were sleeping at odd hours, and you wished people were being quiet when you were sleeping at odd hours. My little flashlight attached to a carabiner came in very handy—I would hook it to my purse strap and use it when I needed to put things away in the dark room or find my toothbrush, etc.

Something I learned very quickly was the value of networking with fellow travelers. A few people told me about a website called Xoom.com, where you could transfer money from your US bank account to various pickup locations around the city. The exchange rate was much better than what you would get at an ATM. I was skeptical at first, but the site turned out to be absolutely amazing—user friendly, secure, etc. Without delay, I sent myself some money and picked it up right down the street. Winning!

All said, I was having a great time and feeling so fortunate to have this opportunity. I met so many amazing people during that first week, including folks from Australia, Finland, England, France, Germany, Bulgaria, Italy, USA, Ecuador, Ireland, Argentina, Canada, Holland, Brazil, Venezuela, Chile, and I'm sure more countries that I forget.

My intensive Spanish classes kicked off the second week in Buenos Aires, and the first week of class went well! It was a bit challenging to get up and go in the morning considering the nights ended so late. Dinner was typically around 10:00 PM, and 2:00 AM was considered an early bedtime.

This lifestyle caught up with me quickly and I became a bit cranky and overtired at one point during my second week away. Feeling desperate for some rest, I took some Advil PM, put in my earplugs, put on my face mask, and crawled into bed around 11:00 PM one night. Funny how this absurdly early bedtime by Argentinian standards would be late for me back home. Regardless, it did me some good as I felt much better the following day.

Each day, I set off for school with my notebook, pen, and an eagerness to learn. There were five other students in my class—two Americans, a Swiss couple, and a Korean. They were all quality people and we would encourage each other, while also laughing at our speaking mishaps. For four hours a day, we took turns reading out loud. Speaking English was not allowed, so we spoke only in Spanish, and it was amazing to see our progress over time.

One of my classmates, Emily, an American woman my age, had also heard about the strategy of going over to Uruguay to get USD. We discussed the potential of going together as the exchange rate had reached a record in Argentina (in our favor) and US dollars were like gold. Even though I still had my emergency stash of a few hundred USD, I needed to conserve that and replenish my disposable funds.

My new school held an optional movie night one evening, and they showed a movie called Nueve Rienas (Nine Queens). The movie was in Spanish with English subtitles, and I found it quite entertaining. The school provided popcorn and my classmates and I brought some beers to drink during the movie. It struck me how drinking was even 'allowed'—I kept finding myself having realizations that there were so many more rules back in America. It would be looked down upon if I strolled into movie night at school in America with a six pack and cracked one open.

Anyway, I was trying my best to pick up the language quickly, so attending extracurricular events like this one really helped. It was a nice time and a great exercise in immersing myself in Spanish! During my first week of class, I also made sure to purchase a Spanish/English dictionary for my studies (a small one that could fit in my backpack of course!).

It didn't take long for me to notice that my eating habits were becoming terrible during the beginning of my trip. I had gained some weight since arriving, primarily driven by an evil empanada place located directly downstairs from the hostel. It was all too convenient, and at about $1.00 for a delicious empanada, I got myself into some trouble there! Not to mention the hostel breakfasts of pure carbohydrates and sugar.

In an effort to stop the madness, I started buying fruits and vegetables from a local shop. My classmates and I also discovered a fantastic lunch spot near our school where you could get a delicious, fresh salad for 26 pesos, which was less than $2.00. This became my regular lunch spot. As opposed to going out for dinner each night, I started making more meals at the hostel. There was a great kitchen atmosphere, with everyone combining their food while cooking, joking, practicing Spanish, and exchanging travel tips and stories.

A huge bonus of being in Argentina was that you could get a magnum of decent vino tinto (red wine) for 20 pesos (about $1.50!). Needless to say, the vino consumption may have been a bit excessive on occasion, which I'm sure also contributed to my expanding waistline!

As far as practical matters went during my second week away, I dropped off laundry for the first time, as having your clothes laundered is apparently the norm while on the road. For a large basket of clothes, I paid about $2.00—certainly not complaining about those prices! While I found the items I had packed to be sufficient, I wished I had brought a heavy sweater, a larger purse, and another pair of jeans. However, I could buy these things locally, so it wasn't really a big deal.

Unfortunately, as far as any potential income went, I learned that the hostel was fully staffed for a while. I considered trying to find work at another hostel, but I really liked the one I was at and felt like it was my home in Buenos Aires. I loved the terraces and common spaces, and most of all, the people I met there.

During my daily routine in Buenos Aires, I managed to get in lots of Spanish practice, but it was tough to find the time to do homework and study. This stressed me out a bit, as I was always a very diligent, high-achieving student! All in all, though, I was very happy as my first couple of weeks on a new continent came to a close!

11

UNEXPECTED ROMANCE

While I did not go into this trip looking for love, I was open to possibilities. I mean, who doesn't fantasize about meeting a hot foreign lover abroad?! I figured I might meet some men along the way, but had no expectations. What I certainly did not expect was to meet someone right away.

One evening during my first week in Buenos Aires, as I walked onto the roof terrace, I spotted Gianfranco—a very tall, handsome, brooding Italian casually smoking a cigarette. Something about him immediately struck me as we locked eyes, and I just knew that something would ultimately transpire between us. His height was undoubtedly a draw, and I liked his full mop of tousled brown hair.

Being the degenerate smoker that I was at the time, I quickly worked up some courage, walked over to him, pulled out a cigarette, and asked him for a light (in very clear and slow English). He still hadn't spoken a word and was quietly analyzing me. He lit my cigarette and simply asked, "Do you always speak like that?" referring to my deliberate words. I said "Sometimes."

As we smoked, we exchanged the basic information that travelers do: names, nationalities, general travel situation. Gianfranco's English was pretty good, but not great, which I found very attractive—there is just something about broken English spoken in an accent . . .

Gianfranco had been on the road for a few months at that point, while I was totally green. We got to chatting, which turned into sharing a beer (the beers they sold at the hostel were massive and very conducive to sharing). As we sipped our beer out of the hostel's dingy communal plastic cups, I felt like he was staring into my soul through his large, wide set eyes. There was a very clear attraction and chemistry between us and while we went our separate ways that night (and did not even kiss!), I knew that we both looked forward to our next meeting.

Even though my first weeks in Buenos Aires were busy with school and social activities, I was still able to carve out a significant amount of time for my new love interest. After our first meeting on the terrace, we reunited at the hostel's weekly asado and continued to get to know one another. That night, we shared our first kiss and he asked me out on a date.

A couple of nights later, we went to a strange, Cirque du Soleil-type show called Fuerza Bruta per his recommendation. The show was crazy—it took place in a nightclub-like atmosphere, with people crowded into a huge dark room surrounded by strobe lights and blasting music. In the middle of the room, various strange scenes played out, from a man sprinting on a massive treadmill to people swimming in clear plastic bubbles that descended from the ceiling. All kinds of aerial feats were performed as music and fog pumped through the venue.

After the show, Gianfranco and I continued our date night over dinner and drinks in Palermo, a very hip neighborhood that I had been dying to check out.

Gianfranco and I were quite smitten with one another right off the bat and started to do practically everything together. Walking around the city hand in hand, stopping for cappuccino breaks, became a daily pastime. In the evenings, Gianfranco would cook delicious Italian feasts while I drank wine and observed. Afternoons were commonly spent together on the terrace studying.

On one of these afternoons, Gianfranco introduced me to maté, a typical Argentinian drink that is similar to tea, yet more bitter. Maté is consumed out of a special cup and straw, and Argentinians carry their personal maté cups, straws, and hot water thermoses around with them everywhere. Gianfranco showed me how to drink it out of the typical cup and straw. Since he was always up earlier than me in the mornings, he would save me medialunas from breakfast as they always went quick. It was a simple, but sweet gesture, and he quickly learned that food is a surefire way to my heart.

Gianfranco was older than me by about eight to ten years. He seemed wise, experienced, and street smart, probably a result of his wide-ranging travels. He was very observant and quietly contemplative—a man of few words. His general demeanor was serious, so when he smiled, it was dazzling. He was disciplined and stuck to routines, one of which was swimming at a local pool on a regular basis. Like me, Gianfranco lived out of a backpack, so had few items of clothing. His standard uniforms consisted of either cargo shorts and a T-shirt, or jeans and a nice sweater.

I adored Gianfranco's way of speaking English. When he was annoyed with himself for struggling with a word or phrase, he would proclaim, "Fuck! My English!" which always made me laugh. When he said he was "sweeting" instead of sweating, I never corrected him because I liked it. However, when he figured out that he wasn't saying it correctly from someone else, he became upset with me for not telling him.

I never actually understood exactly what Gianfranco did for a living but it was some kind of white-collar office job and that was enough to know. He was certainly not satisfied with it. In fact, he seemed very bitter about his career, which did not strike me as odd coming from someone I had met on the traveling circuit. He also seemed disenchanted with the government and corruption in Italy. Among other random facts, he informed me that blonde women were highly desired in Italy due to their rarity, and many corrupt, important men had a blonde by their side.

When I went to pick up cash from my Xoom.com order, Gianfranco offered to come with me so that I felt safer, which was really nice. While I felt comfortable doing this on my own, I would be lying if I said that having a six-foot-seven man with me didn't make me feel a bit more secure.

To wrap up my first week in the city, Gianfranco and I visited the famous San Telmo market. Even though it was a rainy day, it was still wonderful. We did some shopping, had several cappuccinos, and had lunch at an excellent parilla that went by two names—'Parilla de Fredy' and 'Nuestra Parilla.' I had a massive steak sandwich and half of a chorizo sandwich. The meat was insanely delicious and was even better when topped with the mouthwatering chimichurri sauce that was served with it.

According to Gianfranco, I was served a bigger portion because of my blonde hair . . . worked for me! The walls of the parilla were plastered with hand-written notes and memorabilia, so Gianfranco added a note to the wall to mark our time there.

12

NOMAD LIFE

Not to beat a dead horse, but I was really keeping busy at the beginning of my trip and getting up to a variety of things. Something that featured prominently in my new lifestyle was café culture. There were cafés everywhere, with people relaxing and drinking coffee at little tables on the sidewalks. This was definitely one of my new favorite pastimes and I often found myself sitting at the cutest little cafés drinking espresso.

Hanging around with an Italian that liked to drink several espressos a day was beginning to make me fear that I, myself, was developing a habit. I started noticing the flagship 'Illy' sign and stopping for a cortado even when I was alone.

I finally got around to taking the public transport in Buenos Aires, both the bus and subway (known as the Subte). The bus system was different than what I knew at home and I was glad to have Gianfranco with me to navigate my first trip. You needed to tell the driver where you were going, and he or she would then determine the fare based on your destination. It was a bit intimidating to take the bus because I was not yet very confident about my Spanish speaking skills (but I was definitely improving).

To improve my skills, I went to Conversation Club at my school, another helpful extracurricular. There were also many different language exchanges around Buenos Aires through organizations like Mundo Lingo, couchsurfing, etc. that I learned about through talking to people at the hostel. The exchanges were usually held at bars and were a great way to meet new people and practice a new language.

One night, I attended a Mundo Lingo conversation exchange at a bar. During this gathering, people wore stickers of their native country's flag and the flags of any countries with a language that they would like to practice. I wore a US flag and an Argentinian flag. I had a few beers and chatted with some locals but did not stay very long as I quickly learned that these things are 'pick up spots' where the locals are basically trying to meet foreign women.

A few weeks into my overall journey, I took my first side trip to Colonia del Sacramento, Uruguay. I did this for a few reasons: 1. For some R&R (even though I had only been in Buenos Aires for two weeks, the exhaustion from school and late nights was wearing on me), 2. To visit a new country and see a beautiful colonial town, 3. For a money run.

As I've touched on, many people would travel to Uruguay from Argentina to get USD, which they would then exchange on the street in Argentina for a better rate than they would get if they simply withdrew cash from an ATM. By that time, I had met many people at my hostel that had done a money run and many others that wanted to do one. I ended up making the trip with an Australian guy, Robert, and a Dutch girl, Anne, both really fun, cool people that I had been hanging out with at the hostel. They only stayed in Colonia for one day (while I planned to stay the entire weekend for that R&R!), but what a day it was!

We hopped on the morning ferry for the quick ride over to Colonia and hit the streets in search of an ATM. Initially, Robert and Anne had some issues withdrawing money, so we visited every ATM in town to see if they would have any success. As we walked, Robert quipped, "We are taking a bank tour of Colonia," as Anne and I laughed hysterically! My comrades finally figured out that they could get the USD if they withdrew a smaller amount at a time.

Once we all completed our banking tasks, we indulged in huge, local sandwiches (chivitos) and beers for lunch, then walked around exploring the adorable, coastal, cobblestoned town. To wrap up the day, we grabbed some beers at the local supermarket and sat in a park on the water to watch the sun set over a backdrop of sailboat masts and fishing boats. It was truly a glorious day in a beautiful place with great company. We had some genuine, quality laughs which filled my soul with happiness.

I am the type of person that needs laughter in my life and when I find people that can legitimately supply it, I value that more than most other things in the world. It was so nice to meet people with whom I could truly connect.

After sunset, Robert and Anne headed back to Buenos Aires on the ferry and I chose to spend the night at a hostel called El Viajero (The Traveler). I wound up with two German roommates, a guy and a girl that were friends traveling together, who seemed very nice, but I didn't get to know them well in my short time there. The next day, I popped into a few museums, relaxed in some parks, and had an extraordinary cheese/charcuterie/wine lunch with a French girl I had just met in a park.

This particular girl recognized me from the hostel as we were sitting in the park enjoying the seaside ambiance. She said hello in Spanish and we continued to speak to one another in Spanish, even though it was neither of our first languages. We were really hitting it off, so I told her about the wine and cheese place where I intended to have lunch. I had my heart set on this place as it got great reviews and looked adorable when I walked by to scope it out in advance.

She asked if I minded if she joined me and of course I didn't mind—it was lovely to meet a friendly fellow solo woman traveler to have some conversation with. What an unforgettable lunch we had! It was one of the best experiences of my trip to that point. We spoke only in Spanish, yet somehow managed to really bond, laugh, and understand each other. I had three glasses of wine (this was not my original intent . . . I had ordered the 'tasting' which turned out to be three full glasses!) and several varieties of decadent meats and cheeses.

The restaurant itself was reminiscent of a cave, a bit dark and damp, with stone walls, arched doorways, and low ceilings. Racks of wine lined the walls and candles flickered on the tables. It was actually a very romantic setting. Me encanta (I loved it)!!! After lunch, I caught the 4:30 PM ferry back to Buenos Aires. I loved Colonia and HIGHLY recommend visiting there if you ever get the chance!

Back at home base, I thought about how I would stay a bit longer than originally planned as I wanted some time to enjoy the city without the responsibility of having to go to class every day. It should be apparent by now that I had settled in nicely to Buenos Aires.

After two weeks of class, I concluded my Spanish studies. My plan was to take more lessons in another city along my journey, but two weeks was enough for starters. I had a good base and planned to study the material on my own and speak more to improve my skills.

In addition to the trip to Uruguay, I made several other moves within Buenos Aires (even within the hostel itself). Once you leave the hostel, you lose your spot and have to take what you can get if and when you come back. Upon my return from Colonia, I ended up on the first floor of the original hostel in a top bunk in a mixed dorm as that was the only thing available. It wasn't so bad, but definitely messier than the girls' dorm.

I was planning to move to a trendier area of town the following week considering I had finished my classes and wanted to experience a new neighborhood. My move would take me to Palermo, an area full of cute parks, shops, cafés, and bars. One day, I took a walk around the neighborhood to assess potential accommodations and choose a hostel that I liked.

As I was seeking out my new home, I made a few pitstops in cafés and bars to use their WiFi for research and directions. Of course, I ate like a queen while I was at it—lots of meat and pastries. Frankly, I felt like I was going to turn into a tub of dulce de leche.

My plan at that point was to spend a couple of weeks in Palermo before making my way to Iguazu Falls, which is on the border of Argentina, Paraguay, and Brazil. Iguazu Falls is north of Buenos Aires, and my original (albeit very loose) itinerary did not have it factored in. However, I wanted to spend some time with Gianfranco before we parted ways and we had discussed taking this side trip together. I figured that after I visited Iguazu, I would head back down south and start making my way to Patagonia, a 'must see' on my list.

Initially, I thought of flying from Buenos Aires to El Calafate when the time came, but a number of fellow travelers recommended some desirable alternatives. One possibility was to take a bus to Puerto Madryn, stay there for a few days, and then take another bus to El Calafate.

The bus rides to all of the aforementioned places are around seventeen to twenty hours each in duration, but you can book a 'cama' seat, which is a seat that fully reclines and turns into a bed. The busses also serve meals and make frequent stops to ease the pain of the full day of travel. I had a feeling that things were going to get interesting in no time.

With regards to logistics, I exchanged my newly acquired USD for Argentinian pesos in the streets. There is a pedestrian-only street in downtown Buenos Aires called Calle Florida, where many people shout 'Cambio, cambio!' as you walk by. This means 'Change, change!' and you inquire with one of these shouting characters about the exchange rate they are offering. Once you find a suitable business partner, you follow them into a magazine kiosk, shoe store, office, or other shady location to exchange money.

There is a risk of getting fake bills in this kind of situation but all of my transactions turned out to be legit (well, as legit as changing money in the bowels of a magazine stand goes). Keeping track of money was difficult, but I tried to record everything I spent. I did this the old-fashioned way, carrying around a tiny, leather bound notebook in which I wrote journal entries and reconciled my bank balance.

The items that I purchased in Buenos Aires were generally very cheap and the exchange rate situation definitely helped the cause, but I was already thinking about ways to save more money and extend my stay. I thought about getting a TEFL certification online and teaching English for a bit, but I needed a little break from any sort of classes after just having finished two intensive weeks of Spanish!

I registered with workaway.com, which is a website tailored to people who are traveling abroad and looking for temporary work. I was envious of the many people I met from around the world that took sabbaticals regularly and I was plotting ways to be able to do the same!

13

FINAL WEEKS IN BUENOS AIRES

My final weeks in Buenos Aires were action-packed (shocking, right?!). One evening, while having some beers on the hostel's terrace, a group of newcomers arrived— nine English folks that were visiting from São Paulo to attend the New Zealand vs. Argentina rugby game. The people in this group were teachers living in Sao Paulo for indeterminate lengths of time. They offered up extra tickets, and a few of us from the hostel ended up going to the game with them.

Transportation to the game turned out to be a bit of a logistical nightmare, but the game itself was a great time. Gianfranco, our new friend Noah, and I set off to meet our new English friends at the game, but we encountered an obstacle along the way. We tried to take a bus, but the line for the bus was so long that we ended up sharing a taxi with a nice Peruvian girl we recruited from the bus line. Since we had to be there at a certain time to meet up for the tickets, we offered the girl a discount on her share of the fare if we could go directly to the stadium. She obliged.

On the way home, we saved some money by taking a long bus ride. The stadium was in La Plata, about an hour and a half outside of Buenos Aires, and the bus ride home was very cheap for such a long ride (I believe it cost around 20-30 pesos, which is $2.00 max).

In La Plata, we met the English crew and gathered in the park across the street from the stadium to pregame. We all got huge beers and drank them in the park beforehand as drinking is prohibited in the stadium there. At the game, we had the opportunity to see the Haka, which is the famous dance the New Zealand All Blacks perform.

The rugby match (my first ever) was a lot of fun and some locals shared their maté with me during the game, so it was a true Argentinian experience. After the game, while killing time before our bus departed, we had some choripan (meat) and more huge beers (and I wondered why I was gaining weight . . .).

When we returned home that night, we learned that an unfortunate incident had occurred while we were at the game —an Asian guy new to the hostel got robbed via the 'bird shit trick.' He really should have known better (I read about this trick before my trip during my due diligence), but I felt really sorry for him nonetheless. Basically, a couple sprayed some 'bird shit' (probably white paint) on him secretly, then acted like they were going to help him clean it up. They said, "Hand me your bag and we will help you clean it." He handed the bag over, and they ran off with it.

With the additional time on my hands that I was origi-nally spending in school, I was able to visit several museums and other sights. I went to a museum of Latin American art and the Museum of Modern Art (MAMBA). One day I visited a Japanese Garden, and stumbled across a Chilean street fair. Of course, there were the usual café breaks, involving cortados and tostadas (toasted ham and cheese sandwiches), a very typical snack in the area. As usual, I did lots of walking around the city and even took a salsa class with some friends.

I saw my second Spanish movie (Gianfranco's influence—I never would've thought to hit the movie theater on my own). It was a flick about Che Guevara and cost 8 pesos (50 cents) to see. Since this movie did not have subtitles, it was another great way to immerse myself in Spanish. Before departure to the cinema, I made some popcorn in the hostel to bring along as I had learned that this was something that people commonly did. The widespread availability and popularity of my favorite snack of all time (popcorn) in Buenos Aires made me very happy.

On a beautiful Sunday, I returned to the famous San Telmo market so I could experience it on a nice day. As I was walking along, perusing the unusual wares for sale (everything from vintage telephones to modern jewelry), I heard some music and saw a crowd forming. To my delight, there was a tango performance happening in the street. It was such a treat as it can be very expensive to see a proper tango show and these street performers simply collected donations with a hat.

After the day at the market, it was off to dinner at a Peruvian restaurant featured in my Lonely Planet guide, called Chan Chan. I had been hyping the place up to Gianfranco and when our dinner was served, there was a hair in his food. Typical! The food was otherwise great, though, and we feasted on some fantastic ceviche and another dish of perfectly dressed fish. It felt good to finally eat something healthy and I looked forward to a ceviche-filled future in Peru.

Usually on Sundays back home I would get a case of the 'Sunday Scaries.' However, I no longer felt that old familiar sense of dread surrounding the week ahead. Now, Mondays were really no different from weekend days.

In fact, I went to a concert on a Monday, which is something I wouldn't normally do back home. I met a newcomer in the hostel and recruited him to come with me to the show, which was called La Bomba. It was a percussion show that I had heard a lot about from others at the hostel and at Spanish school.

My new recruit was named Jacob, and he was from Germany. Jacob spoke little, if any, Spanish, so I helped him obtain a Sube card (local transport card) with my newly acquired language skills. While I was still timid, I knew I had to put myself in situations where I needed to speak the language. It was good that I had to help Jacob, as I was lazy when I was with friends that could speak Spanish really well, allowing them to do all the talking.

At the percussion show, we ran into some others from the hostel—an American guy and an Irish couple. We all hung out together and had a really fun time, heading back to the hostel together for a dinner of pizza and empanadas. When I told Gianfranco about how I did most of the communicating earlier in the evening since my Spanish was the best, he created a Spanish award for me by drawing on a piece of paper. It's funny how little things like that end up being the meaningful mementos that you save.

It wasn't all rainbows and awards though, as I realized that Gianfranco was quite jealous of my new friend Jacob. He made his place known by saying something a bit territorial later in the evening to Jacob. It was not a big deal, but I was embarrassed by his behavior. I took Jacob aside later and explained my relationship with Gianfranco and thankfully, he was very understanding.

Up to that point, Gianfranco and I had been keeping our 'relationship,' if you could call it that, under wraps. Not because we had anything to hide, but because there was no need to flaunt it around when it could hinder us from meeting new people. However, the lack of privacy in our current living situation eventually got old. Not only is it awkward, but it's also rude to fool around or sleep two to a bed in a dorm room!

Gianfranco worked in the hostel so we had inside knowledge of unoccupied rooms (and access to keys!) so we would steal moments alone wherever we could but it wasn't easy. So, we decided to make a temporary move together and moved to a new place in the San Telmo neighborhood for a change of scenery for a couple days. I have to confess that while I was happy to have the privacy, I missed my original hostel family.

The new place, called Art Factory, had a very hip vibe—it was plastered with modern art from floor to ceiling in every room. Even the fixtures fit with the modern art theme. The place was a maze of vivid color, but it didn't feel 'homey' to me. It was important to branch out, though—my trip was supposed to be all about experiencing new things!

During this little hiatus within a hiatus, Gianfranco and I continued to explore the seemingly boundless city. One trip took us to the Chinatown neighborhood ('Barrio Chino'), where we slipped in and out of shops filled with oriental spices and wares. Our travels also took us back to Chan Chan, the Peruvian restaurant, for more ceviche (no hair in the food this time!).

We strolled hand in hand through Las Caminitas, a colorful, historical neighborhood in an area called La Boca. This walk also took us by La Bombanera, the stadium of the La Boca Juniors football team which people were obsessed with. Because this neighborhood can be dangerous, we made sure to visit during the day. I knew it could be dangerous due to the research I had done on the city, and also from talking with fellow travelers—I can't stress enough how important it is to learn about your surroundings and ensure that you don't put yourself in unsafe situations!

Safety concerns aside, it was really nice to have someone

whose company I enjoyed and with whom I could explore. Of course, no day was complete without several stops at cafés for espresso. During one of these stops, Gianfranco presented me with a gift—a bracelet I had seen at the San Telmo market when we went there together. I had decided not to buy it for myself, but he had returned on his own to get it for me, which was very thoughtful.

While I enjoyed spending time with Gianfranco and it was hard to peel myself away, I knew it was too early in my trip to get seriously attached. Therefore, I made sure to create time for myself. In order to do the soul searching I had set out to do, I had to spend some time alone.

To clear my head, I walked through the ecological reserve frequently. Its seaside location must have had a calming effect on me. I needed this respite as I started to notice over time that Gianfranco had a tendency toward jealousy. He commented that I dressed up extra nice when I went out with other people and wondered why I didn't do that for him. This was kind of appalling considering I literally had about three outfits!

He also made a comment about my drinking habits. While I certainly drank more than I would in normal, everyday life back home, I didn't think I drank *that* much. Gianfranco informed me that Italian women drank very little, though. I reminded him that I was not an Italian woman and that he should not be commenting on my personal choices. Simultaneously, I made a mental note to self that this would never work out in the long run, and I would just enjoy it while it lasted.

This was all swirling through my mind when Gianfranco casually suggested getting an apartment together in Buenos Aires for a month or so. His reasoning was fair—we could probably find a place for a decent price where we wouldn't have to deal with other peoples' messes. However, I knew that it was too soon for me to settle down in any way, shape, or form. Buenos Aires was the first stop on my trip and I intended to make it to several other places. Fortunately, Gianfranco was very understanding.

When I emailed my girlfriends to catch up, noting this latest development with Gianfranco, one of my friends responded, "DO NOT MOVE IN WITH THAT MAN." When I read it, I was consumed with laughter!

A highlight of those last few weeks in Buenos Aires included the privilege of attending a show at Teatro Colon, one of the premier opera houses in the world. Teatro Colon offered a free Sunday show each week but you needed to get tickets in advance. Acquiring the free tickets involved waking up very early on Friday morning and waiting in line at the theater for two hours. I went on this ticket acquisition mission with my Boston friend, Nicole. We were able to secure four tickets each, and ultimately, eight of us from the hostel attended the show on Sunday.

The wait was worthwhile, as the theater itself was glorious inside and the music was beautiful. The domed ceiling, painted with beautiful murals, was reminiscent of the Sistine Chapel and for a moment, I felt like a classy lady instead of a backpacker.

It should come as no surprise that there were plenty of memorable meals during those last few weeks in Buenos Aires, both inside and outside of the hostel. On taco night at the hostel, I even made a contribution that I was proud of— my famous guacamole. A new American hostel guest, Dave, was a chef by trade and he cooked up a lovely meal for a group of us one evening. Gianfranco cooked several nice dinners as I 'supervised' (a.k.a. drank wine and washed a few dishes).

I continued to consume obscene amounts of medialunas and red meat. There were sidewalk parilla lunches and decadent Indian dinner feasts. On one of my final Friday nights, I went to an outstanding parilla called 'Parilla Peña,' which was recommended by my Spanish teacher. There, I had a topnotch meal with two new Dutch friends, Anne and Eric.

While the availability of diverse, delicious food in Buenos Aires was impressive, the hostel breakfasts were disappointing. I quickly got sick of white bread rolls topped with crap and cornflakes. These are things I would not typically eat at home, but that I ate because the hostel breakfast was free and I wanted to conserve funds. It was frustrating that the healthiest option for breakfast was a bowl of cornflakes. Mind you, these cornflakes came from an industrial sized bag that was untidily shoved onto a kitchen shelf for storage when not in use. Not to mention the milk that came from a huge communal jug that would sit around for hours on the breakfast table.

I justified eating this terrible stuff with all of the walking I was doing. I also finally made it a point to squeeze in a few Rocky-style workouts on the rooftop of the hostel. One day, I worked out with two American girls who were on a short holiday and not letting themselves go like I was! They motivated me and we did a HIIT workout that included thirty second intervals of burpees, pushups, lunges, etc.

In addition to the walking and the rooftop workouts, I took a few more bike rides around the ecological reserve in Puerto Madero. While I was too paranoid to ride the bikes anywhere else due to traffic, I planned to get a few rides in when I moved over to Palermo, as there were many nice parks there.

One of the more unique dining experiences I had during my time in Buenos Aires was attending a 'puerto cerrado' (closed door) dinner, a secret dinner party in someone's house that has been partially transformed into a restaurant. You don't know where it is or how much it costs until you reserve it. There is no sign on the door and an air of secrecy and exclusivity surrounds the whole experience. I was invited by a girl I met in Spanish class, Emily.

Emily and her boyfriend, John, were from the United States and were living temporarily in Buenos Aires. They were cool people—they were from California and exuded that laid back Cali vibe. Emily, a pretty brunette, gave off a bohemian air and John, a handsome Asian American, gave off a smart, clean cut one. Emily and John invited me to their apartment to meet up before dinner and the visit provided an interesting perspective on a different mode of traveling. While I was bouncing from hostel to hostel, Emily and John had a dedicated space for themselves in a trendy neighborhood.

I felt a pang of jealousy upon seeing their place. It was hip, homey, large, and had closets instead of backpacks as storage units. The closets held a variety of clothing . . . much more than my quick dry pants and athletic wear. I found myself envying their decision to live in Buenos Aires. While I had made a similar decision, I was executing my travels in a different manner—I was not living in an apartment and settling in like they were. However, I soon realized that I was being very hard on myself, which was something that was basically programmed into my DNA and that I knew I needed to work on.

Back to the evening at hand . . . we had a drink at their place and proceeded to the secret restaurant, where we indulged in a fabulous multi-course Asian fusion meal. Flawless, fluffy crab cakes and fresh spring rolls, each accompanied by a perfectly paired sauce were a few of the highlights.

The night continued at a classy bar in Palermo. I didn't feel like a backpacker that night and it gave me such mixed feelings. On one hand, I was loving the fancy night out but on the other, I was thinking—am I spending too much money?? Is this an authentic experience?? Or I am just doing things that are familiar to me??

There was no rest for the weary as my adventures continued. I took a solo day trip to Tigre, a small town of canals about an hour and a half outside of Buenos Aires. There, I took a boat ride to explore the canals during the beautiful sunny day. It was a nice break from the city that allowed me some time to collect my thoughts.

Alone time was very difficult to come by, which may come as a surprise. It certainly came as a surprise to me—when I initially embarked on this solo trip, I thought it was possible that I would have the opposite problem (i.e. being lonely). This was definitely not the case. When you are staying in hostels and participating in group activities, you are constantly surrounded by other people. In fact, you need to become comfortable telling others that you are going off to bed to read and not feel guilty about leaving the party when you need some time to yourself.

Gianfranco and I spent yet more time taking in the city together. We went to watch tango in a park in Belgrano, where many people dance in the evenings. With Quilmes (local beer) tall boys in hand, we stood on the edge of the gazebo spectating. At one point, an old man whom I learned was a professor of tango, grabbed me from the sidelines and showed me a few steps. I felt lucky to get a free tango lesson and knew it was because of my blonde hair. My hair color stood out and people would stare at me in the streets which is something I had to get used to.

As those final weeks continued on, I squeezed in even more . . . I walked around the beautiful parks of Palermo a few times. It was springtime so the geese and ducks were having their babies, making the parks feel extra special. I checked a few more museums off the list, namely Bicentennario and Fortabat. Finally, I took in a tango show and lesson on my last night in the city with a new friend from the hostel.

It wasn't all fun and games during those last few weeks in Buenos Aires and there was one pretty terrible part. I had a bed bug incident (henceforth referred to simply as 'the incident'), which officially ruined two days of my trip. I had just moved over to a hostel in the 'fancy neighborhood' of Palermo. After waking up one morning with several bug bites, I tried to maintain composure as I took my iPad to the communal breakfast area to google bed bug bite images.

I quickly confirmed the situation I was dealing with, packed my bag at the most rapid rate I have ever packed a bag, and evacuated the room. Discreetly, I told the receptionist about what happened and the hostel was pretty good about helping me by paying for all of my laundry to be done and helping to clean my bags just in case any of the bugs made their way in there.

Before I sent out my laundry, I went to a local shop and purchased a new outfit so that I could put literally every piece of clothing that was exposed into the laundry. I picked out a pair of jeans and a tank top that didn't fit perfectly but I was desperate. Then, I literally scrubbed the crevices of my sneakers because I was so worried about transporting the bed bugs with me.

Once I sorted out the laundry and cleaning situation, I had to get some itch cream and anti-histamines because the bites were extremely itchy and swollen. Mind you, a trip to the pharmacy was not as simple as you might think—you can't just walk in and grab something off a shelf—you need to speak to the pharmacist to get anything, even aspirin. This meant I needed to figure out how to say 'itch cream' and 'anti-histamines' in Spanish, which of course I did, but my point is that it takes a lot more preparation to visit a store when you are in a Spanish-speaking country and not fluent in the language!

To wrap up this disturbing piece of my tale, I had a few unpleasant days of wanting to tear my skin off, but all is well that ends well. Gianfranco was very sweet, comforting me about the whole situation while also being realistic, saying "Kerie, this will not be the only time this happens to you. This has happened to me. It is very bad, but it happens to everyone who travels."

After the 'incident,' I moved backed to my original home, Hostel Estoril. Gianfranco assisted me with the big move. He even bought me a flower, which I put into a water bottle as a makeshift vase to decorate my new space.

I moved into a new room where there was an ever present strange, rude, noisy man. This guy would yawn very loudly, turn lights on, listen to music, talk on the phone, blow snot rockets, etc. while everyone was sleeping. He left his wet towel on my bed one day and that was basically the last straw for me in that room. The joys of hostel life!

By the end of my time in Buenos Aires, I had slept in approximately twelve beds. I have to admit, I was tired of avoiding other peoples' hair in the shower, questioning how filthy my dishes were, dealing with sloppy roommates, and so on. One day the hostel did not have water, so I had to skip my daily shower. I employed the good old trusty wipe-down with wet wipes for that day's shower. I thought about looking into Airbnb and some other lodging options once I arrived at the next destination where I would spend any considerable time.

My next few stops (Iguazu, Puerto Madryn, El Calafate, El Chalten) would be temporary enough to stay in hostels. I heard the hostels were much nicer in those places than they were in the big city, which allayed some of my newfound bed bug fears.

As I've alluded to, I was finding some facets of hostel life to be exhausting and challenging after a few weeks. I was coming down with a little head cold and I knew it was due to being around sick people in the hostel who didn't exactly practice perfect hygiene. They would use the shared hand towels in the bathrooms and would not wash their dishes properly. I was most certainly not a germophobe, but I think that having to eat out of poorly washed communal dishes would skeeve anyone out.

To combat these issues, I started to use my small quick dry towel instead of the shared ones in the bathrooms, I started to wash all dishes before using them, and I purchased my own breakfast food more often.

I was also a bit tired of constantly having to lock my belongings up, even for a five-minute trip to the bathroom. While there were some minor inconveniences in my life, I realized that these small sacrifices were part of life on the road, and the bigger picture made it all worth it.

A disheartening reality presented itself as I prepared to leave Buenos Aires—I would have to say goodbye to people that had become friends and make new friends on a regular basis. Even though it is easy to meet people on the traveling circuit, the constant retelling of your 'story' while learning others' stories can wear on you.

As my departure neared, some new friends I wondered about 'how the movie would end' for all of us. Of course, I didn't know how my own movie would end and there was beauty in that. I truly looked forward to the possibilities and what would happen next in my movie.

As usual, logistics needed to be tended to before hitting the road. An important order of business was to buy a spare adapter. Keeping electronics charged had proven to be a challenge as you don't want to leave an expensive iPad or phone around when you can't watch over them. Bus tickets needed to be booked, and the next destination needed to be researched.

After five weeks in the city, I didn't know where the time had gone, but I was about to make my first real move. While I loved the city and could have spent more time there as there were endless things to do, I was excited to move on in my journey and get out of the metropolis for a while to experience some natural beauty. I was slated to head north on a 19-hour bus journey to Iguazu Falls, which is located on the border of Argentina, Brazil, and Paraguay. These falls are some of the most impressive and magnificent in the world.

I booked a 'super cama' seat, which is the best you can book on a bus. It reclines into a full bed and you are served meals, snacks, and wine. I probably could have managed with a 'cama' seat, which reclines 180 degrees, but I would be traveling with Gianfranco, who was very tall, so we figured we better get the good seats! Yes, I was still with Gianfranco and we were leaving Buenos Aires together. However, we planned to make this our farewell trip, and would be parting ways after a few days in Iguazu. Then, I would head south toward Patagonia and he would head into Brazil.

As my time in the city came to an end, I continued to collect tips and tricks from other travelers as we all shared stories and laughs over a few beers or glasses of wine. I thought of some of the particularly special and/or strange things that I did not want to forget about Buenos Aires, including:

- Crossing the widest boulevard in the world on a daily basis (and racing to make it in one go, which I only achieved once or twice)
- Making cambio transactions in the bowels of magazine stands
- Café life

- Medialunas and empanadas and the constant battle to avoid them
- Feeling like a child again in the sense that I was constantly observing and learning about new things around me: the language, noises of the city, customs, modes of transportation, etc.
- The poverty and seeing children sleeping on the street and selling things to patrons at cafés
- The grit
- My daily siesta
- The fact that the 90's were alive and well: rollerblading, rat tails, and big chunky heels were all the rage

14

IGUAZU FALLS

In case you were wondering if I would ever leave Buenos Aires, I finally did, traveling to Puerto Iguazu on a 17-hour overnight bus. The Iguazu Falls are located on the border of Argentina, Brazil, and Paraguay, and are some of the most spectacular in the world. The falls are considered one of the new seven natural wonders of the world (whatever that means) and are comprised of about 275 waterfalls.

While the bus ride was long, it was fairly painless, which could be attributed to my super cama seat and the fact that I slept for a combined total of twelve hours. At the beginning of the bus ride, Gianfranco and I watched The Hobbit to kill some time. Then, we had some dinner and wine, reclined our super cama seats to the flat position, and went to sleep for the night.

The food on the bus was not great—in fact, it was worse than airplane food. Dinner consisted of some mystery meat, jello, mashed pumpkin, and a questionable ham and cheese sandwich. Breakfast included three varieties of cookies.

I was awoken with a start at one point as we traversed some very rough roads which jostled me around in my seat.

This was kind of scary, but aside from that, the ride was quite seamless until we were twenty minutes away from our destination. At that point, the bus broke down. Fortunately, another bus arrived quickly to take us the rest of the way.

We got our first taste of the climate during this bus transfer, which can only be described as VERY HOT. I cannot stress this enough. The heat was oppressive, and the locals said it was hotter than usual for this time of year with temperatures averaging around 105 degrees Fahrenheit with high humidity.

Upon arrival to the town of Puerto Iguazu, Gianfranco and I made our way to a hostel that we had booked for one night in advance. It was in the center of town—a convenient point from which to look around to see where we would ultimately like to stay for the week. Searching for our 'home for the week' proved to be very taxing, as it involved walking around drenched in sweat and getting frustrated about the options.

Once we decided that we would like to stay at our originally booked place, it was too late, as it was already fully reserved for the week. So, more looking around ensued and we finally chose a place a few blocks away. This place was not as good, but it was 'acceptable' in Gianfranco's words.

During the first night in the original hostel, Gianfranco discovered a few huge cockroaches scattering when he turned on the light in the room. He complained to the receptionist only to get a response of "Estas en la selva" ("You are in the jungle"). This was true, and while I've seen cockroaches in many different places in the world, I still did not want them wandering around my bedroom.

The second hostel did not have cockroaches (that we noticed), but had frequent power and internet outages. Apparently, power outages were common occurrences throughout the town, and not the fault of the hostel.

However, these outages were very disappointing when we would come back to no power after daydreaming of air conditioning during our daily excursions.

One night during a regular power outage, I took a shower in the dark, even managing to shave my legs and wash some sweaty clothes in complete darkness. Then, I cooked dinner with a headlamp on—it's surprising what you can do when you need to!

Our first full day in town was all about seeing the falls. We were among the first to arrive at the park at 8:00 AM, as we heard and read that you must get there very early to avoid massive crowds, to avoid extreme heat, and to see the most wildlife. The local bus drivers were on strike that day, resulting in some transport logistics that needed to be worked out, so we almost didn't achieve our goal of arriving early.

Ultimately, we took a taxi, but we needed to find two other people to share the taxi with us in order to keep costs down. We found some French girls from the hostel to share with, so this worked out well (albeit after some schlepping around town debating on how best to recruit partners).

To view the falls while walking, there are two 'circuits' you can do—the upper and lower—and we did both. The waterfalls themselves were very impressive—a true natural wonder to behold! Que lindo (How beautiful)!! There were many tourists so it was difficult to find a solitary moment to appreciate the beauty and take it all in. However, we walked the 'wrong way' intentionally on the catwalks so that we could avoid some of the crowds.

Coatis (animals similar to raccoons) wandered around among the people, seemingly unafraid and interested in acquiring scraps of food. Several signs warned tourists not to feed them, but of course some folks did. Some of these signs showed horrific injuries that could result from a coati attack, so I was hesitant to get too close to them.

For a different perspective, we took an ecological boat tour, which involved boating through the jungle. This wasn't really worth it, as it was extremely hot, mosquito ridden, and did not afford as many opportunities to view wildlife as we thought it would. Next, we decided to try our luck on a different boat ride—one that goes very close to and under some of the falls. This was wet and wild, which was very welcomed in the blazing heat. It was also pretty scary because we went so close to the base of the falls that it felt like we were going to get sucked into them.

Throughout the day, Gianfranco and I took hundreds of pictures of the plentiful, brilliantly colored butterflies (over 200 species of butterflies live in Iguazu) as they landed on our clothes or on the catwalk railings. There were black butterflies with fiery red stripes and dots, brilliant cerulean blue butterflies with geometrically perfect orange spots, white butterflies with black and red accents, and more! Once we had enough action for the day, we returned 'home' for a siesta before venturing out for dinner.

Next up was dinner at an outside market, 'La Feria,' in Puerto Iguazu where vendors hawk products primarily from Mendoza. This is because many Brazilians go there to buy Mendozan products, as they can't get them at home. There were copious amounts of olives, wines, cheeses, oils, beers, sweets, etc. The sheer amount and variety of olives was extraordinary and had me salivating. For this reason, we chose to dine at one of the market's eateries, and ordered picadas (a plate of cheese, olives, and salami) and multiple empanadas.

Gianfranco was a bit worried about the food being out in the heat and commented, "This food could be problematic. We will see within twenty-four hours." I loved his ways of saying certain things in English. Fortunately, the food did not end up being problematic and we even returned to the same place to eat again during our week in Puerto Iguazu.

The market was such a feast for the senses. A man around fifty years old served as the DJ in the midst of a large courtyard, blasting American 80s and Grease soundtrack hits. He had a stereo system with big speakers that appeared to be straight out of the decade of his preferred music. The DJ was really proud of his music selections and kept asking us "Do you like? Do you like?" "Yes!" I said with a smile, but the truth was I couldn't even hear myself think because it was so loud. Hilarious . . .

During Day Two at Iguazu National Park, Gianfranco and I embarked on a seven-kilometer jungle trek on a trail called Sendero Macuco. It was a flat walk, so not very challenging, but the heat was a bit of an issue again. We saw lots of wildlife on this hike and had the trail to ourselves for the most part, which was great. Toward the beginning of our trek, a coati came out of the jungle brush and starting scurrying after us, looking like he was interested in a meal or maybe a camera. I snapped a quick photo of him but then ran away, as I was afraid that he would get aggressive.

We also saw monkeys, many beautiful butterflies, some huge lizards, and the largest ants I have ever seen. When I had to pee on the side of the trail, I was a bit scared, as there was a huge jungle wasp in sight and who knows what kinds of poisonous plants and animals around. The last thing I needed was the sting of a jungle wasp or the jungle equivalent of poison ivy on my bare bum!

We ourselves fit right in as creatures of the jungle— sweaty jungle beasts to be specific. The Sendero Macuco trail culminated at a beautiful, small-for-Iguazu but huge-for-real-life waterfall, where you could swim. Because I did not have the appropriate undergarments on, I just waded in, but crazy Gianfranco decided to go swimming and walk underneath the powerful waterfall. He said he couldn't breathe or see while under the waterfall, and that its force was tremendous. I opted against this dangerous activity and took photos instead!

After some time spent cooling off, we hiked back. Overall, the hike was lovely, and allowed us some time to talk. We talked about some of the differences between America and Italy, life at home vs. life on the road, ideals, goals, etc. Conversations with someone who has a very different background are so interesting and informative, and I really enjoyed learning about the way other parts of the world worked.

The remainder of our days in Puerto Iguazu were spent doing activities around the town. One day, we walked to the 'Tres Fronteras' ('Three Borders,' the border between Paraguay, Argentina, and Brazil) and sat on a bench observing three different countries from one vantage point. Argentina was the only country of these three that I was allowed to visit without a previously arranged visa.

On another day, we visited a place called La Aripuca, a place occupied by large eco-friendly wooden structures built by indigenous people and where we learned about the jungle of Misiones. We also visited an animal refuge called Guira Ogo, which involved yet another long sweaty walk, this one among cages of rescued animals that were being rehabilitated. The place was home to a variety of parrots, toucans, other exotic birds, armadillos, turtles, etc.

On yet another day, we visited a hummingbird garden called Jardin de Picaflores, which was spectacular. A woman with a passion for birds started this little place at her home and eventually turned it into a business (it was only 30 pesos, or $2.00 to visit). She was so friendly and adorable, showing us guides of the jungle wildlife and sitting with us while we observed the hummingbirds.

While in town, we even attended a film festival! As we were walking around, we noticed that there was an international film festival taking place, so we attended that one night. We signed up to watch a movie without knowing what it would be about, and it turned out to be a very graphic, disturbing war flick. The movie was all in Spanish, so I didn't comprehend much of the conversation, but the film was very powerful and well done. I am surprised it didn't give us nightmares, though!

During our time in Puerto Iguazu, Gianfranco and I discovered and frequented a favorite local panaderia (bakery). We drank coffee and ate piles of baked goods (the dulce de leche-filled pastries were my downfall). Of course, we also went for helado (ice cream) many times, justifying this behavior by the constant walking and sweating.

While on this little side trip to Iguazu, we considered visiting the Brazilian side of the falls, but this posed an issue due to the fact that I didn't have a Brazilian visa. A taxi driver that was lingering around the downtown tourism office insisted he could take us there without any problems. He explained that this would involve getting stamped out of Argentina, never stamped into Brazil, and then coming back to Argentina. I read that this was possible but I was nervous about it.

Another man in the tourism office who overheard our conversation said that if I got caught doing it, I would be fined at least $150.00 USD and who knows what else so I decided not to chance it. It probably would not have been an issue, but frankly, I wasn't up for spending the night in a Brazilian prison in the off chance the cab broke down or crashed and the Brazilian officials realized I didn't have any legal documentation.

There was a couple in our hostel facing a similar dilemma . . . the guy was from England, the girl from the US, and she didn't want to chance it either. I could tell that Gianfranco really wanted me to do it, but I did not succumb to the pressure! It was too early on in my trip to be doing stupid things!

As I reflected during my time in Iguazu, I noticed that many of the things that struck me at the very beginning of my trip were no longer novel to me. I continued to meet people from all over the world, learn about myself and my levels of tolerance, use really sketchy bathrooms, sleep in strange places, get better at packing and minimizing, etc.

Now, when I encountered a bathroom with toilet paper, I felt like the place was luxury. If there were also paper towels or a hand dryer, that was a true bonus. Finally, if there was a hook where I could hang my backpack as opposed to placing it on the filthy bathroom floor, I felt like I really hit the jackpot.

With regards to packing, I was able to get rid of some things, which made me feel proud—I purged a long sleeve shirt, a T-shirt, a camisole, two makeup brushes, facewash, and my hair product. This may not sound like a lot, but anything helps when you are carrying around a huge backpack in the heat. I wished I could have dumped more, but I needed clothes to layer when I would be in cold climates. Of course, I didn't just dump these items; I gave them away to people who could use them.

I replaced my facewash with face wipes, as I used them more frequently and there was no sense in having two items that performed the same function. I also bought a bar of laundry soap and started to wash my own clothes more, likely due to Gianfranco's influence. My new self-laundering methods saved laundry trips and helped to avoid schlepping around a backpack full of sweaty clothing.

Gianfranco was a professional budget traveler and I definitely picked up several tips from him. There were certain levels that he took it to that I knew I never would, though. For example, one morning I came out of the room to find him sewing a pair of his socks on the balcony!

After visiting Iguazu, Gianfranco planned to head to Peru, Colombia, and Brazil for the rest of his trip, and while I did not have a concrete itinerary, I knew I would head to Patagonia next. The time we spent together was memorable to say the least.

Toward the end, the extreme heat affected our relationship a bit, making us irritable due to the constant suffering from heat exposure. Taking a side trip with a travel companion was an important experience as it helped me to appreciate the challenges and compromises that come along with traveling with someone else. It can be difficult to share every moment of every day with someone in tight quarters, especially in the jungle heat. In fact, it is quite easy to drive each other a little crazy at times in these circumstances.

Moreover, different people from different places in the world have very different ways of operating, viewing the world, and performing their daily activities. Agreeing on where to stay, what and when to eat, what activities to do, how to get around, etc. can be a test, but in the end, a very good learning experience.

At one point, Gianfranco described me as 'chaotic,' referring to the fact that I was messy with leaving my things around the room. I couldn't stand his slow decision-making process and the fact that he did what I considered too much 'pounding the pavement' before making decisions on where to stay. Ultimately, however, our time spent together was meaningful and I knew I would never forget him.

It was hard to say goodbye when the time came, and we were both quite sad, but such are the realities of life on the road. It was also weird to be alone after having spent over a month with Gianfranco by my side. I left Iguazu independently on a 17-hour bus ride back to Buenos Aires. Gianfranco saw me off and I quietly wept as the bus pulled out of the station.

It was truly bittersweet to say goodbye to a lover while also looking forward to the next chapter in my adventure. During the long ride (and many thereafter), I listened to the diverse music collection that I had downloaded onto my old school iPod shuffle. The eclectic mix of love songs by Jason Aldean, upbeat jams by Pitbull, and sad songs by Coldplay served as the perfect soundtrack to my inner turmoil.

Buenos Aires would be my layover before getting on another long bus ride (twenty hours) to Puerto Madryn, about 1,500 kilometers further south. I was finally learning to speak in kilometers and kilograms (why is America the only place with a different system?!). Argentina is MASSIVE, and there was so much to see. In Puerto Madryn, I planned to meet up with Frederik, a German friend I had met in the original hostel in Buenos Aires.

Frederik was doing an internship in Puerto Madryn, and had told me to pay him a visit if I ended up in that area. While there, I would also visit Peninsula Valdes, home to right whales, penguins, dolphins, elephant seals, sea lions, guanacos, and other very cool wildlife. Fortunately for me, the timing was fantastic, as it was the best time of year to see wildlife, which is one of the main reasons I added this place to my rough itinerary.

After visiting that area, I figured that I would get on another 20-hour bus ride to El Calafate which is in southern Patagonia, but I didn't want to plan too far in advance. I did know that I wanted to visit the glaciers and experience the epic hiking that can be found in the south of Argentina and Chile. Once I did that, my rough itinerary had me heading north to Santiago del Chile, Mendoza, San Pedro de

Atacama, Peru, and hopefully more places before my money ran out!

Budget-wise, I was doing pretty well so far, but the next month or so would involve a lot of transport costs and touristy destinations which meant more spending.

15

PUERTO MADRYN - INTRO TO PATAGONIA

A fter a quick layover in Buenos Aires at my original home, Hostel Estoril, I hopped on a 20-hour bus ride to Puerto Madryn. Puerto Madryn is a town on the northeast coast of Patagonia, famous for its wildlife. The bus ride wasn't bad, but it was not as luxurious as the super cama to Iguazu. This time around, I had a regular cama seat which doesn't fully recline, but I still managed to sleep for a good eight hours or so.

The usual dinner of crappy bus food was served (although I chose the veggie option this time based on a tip from a fellow traveler and it was much better). I also downed some alfajores (delicious Argentinian cookies), Tylenol PM, and red wine to assure sound sleep.

During my one-night layover in Buenos Aires, I managed to get a few massive mosquito or spider bites, so I was itchy for the entirety of the bus ride. My tiger balm came in handy when the itching was unbearable! The bites lasted for ages, but I was happy they were not bed bug bites.

During the bus ride, I caught up on some tour guide reading and Spanish studies, which was nice, because it was nearly impossible to find the time for these things. I studied amidst blasting Beyonce and Britney Spears videos that were playing on the bus televisions. The modes of travel I experienced were quite comical at times.

I was pleasantly surprised with my accommodations upon arrival to the hostel in Puerto Madryn. The place was great except for the bed. The rooms were very clean, the clientele and staff were friendly, and there were views of the ocean from a second-floor balcony. As I sipped my morning coffee, I could see whales from the balcony. The only downside of the place was the bed, which had a massive indent from a million people sleeping on it over time. Ahhh, hostel life.

Puerto Madryn reminded me of home and my true love for the sea. I knew I could never live inland for too long, and it was so refreshing to be in a quaint little beach town. As I mentioned, my new friend Frederik was now living in Puerto Madryn, so we met up on Day One and had a few beers on the beach while watching the whales jump around close to shore. Frederik called out, "Say Whale!" as we took selfies trying to capture a whale's tale in the background. We had some great laughs trying to capture 'the classic' shot. I envied Frederik's ability to joke around and actually be funny in a language that was not his native one. It inspired me to keep studying my Spanish!

Frederik lived in a house on the beach with an Argentinian man named Javier, who happened to be an actor in soap operas and movies (and an overall hilarious character). Javier had a handsome face and long, flowing locks—he basically looked exactly like what you would expect an Argentinian soap opera actor to look like. Javier also worked in tourism and hooked me up with a cheaper than average tour of the penguin colony, Punta Tombo, which was a score.

I had dinner at Javier and Frederik's place on Night One, dining with the two of them and Javier's two kids, who were both around the age of ten. We all spoke Spanish over dinner, which was a great experience. Frederik cooked an excellent meal and I, of course, supervised (stood by drinking wine and being completely useless). He cooked a massive pot of chicken and vegetables in a flavorful sauce, fit to share with an army. The tendency of everyone I met to share and always think of others never ceased to amaze me.

A few nights later, I attended a dinner party at Javier and Frederik's house, which was an awesome experience because everyone was from Argentina and speaking Spanish. The dinner was delicious and we drank copious amounts of red wine as the party attendees taught me new words and phrases. Back at the hostel, I was also speaking Spanish only, which was so good for me! The tourists in my hostel were French and Chinese, so we had to communicate in Spanish as it was our only shared language. I met a friend of Gianfranco's, Domingo, for coffee at one point and he did not speak any English, so that afforded me yet another great practice session. My skills were improving but still needed lots of work!

During my second day in Patagonia, I visited Peninsula Valdes, which is a protected area home to a great deal of wildlife. I participated in a full day tour, which is really the only viable option for visiting this place. While I am not big on commercialized, organized tours, as they are so expensive, I had to see this place. The only other option was to rent a car with a group and I arrived too late to meet people to do this with. This method can also be sketchy with insurance and whatnot (the roads are mainly gravel and pretty much everyone has a cracked windshield).

The tour was the right move anyway—it turned out to be fantastic. During the tour, we visited many points on the peninsula and saw lots of elephant seals, sea lions, guanacos (llama-like animals), maras (largest rodent in Patagonia), rheas (ostrich-like birds), armadillos, various birds, penguins, and more. It was a delight for any nature lover! At one point during the tour, some guanacos surprised and scared me, popping up just feet away, as I was hiking down a short trail on my own! As I crouched down to take a picture of them, an armadillo scurried by . . . naaaaature!

There was an add-on option to go on a whale watch for two hours during the tour, but I skipped this part. I had several reasons for skipping it—it cost around $50.00 USD, I had already seen whales during this trip, and I could see them from shore just fine while sipping a $1.50 espresso and studying Spanish.

On Day Three, I bought a bus ticket to El Calafate. I forgot to specify a veggie meal which was disappointing because even though I will eat pretty much anything, the mystery meat served on the busses was the most questionable food I had encountered thus far on my trip. Speaking of my diet, it was still terrible. The hostel breakfasts continued to be the same—white bread rolls with jam and dulce de leche. I ate a number of these rolls smothered in dulce de leche every day because I needed energy for the day and the options were really limited.

While I could buy things at the supermarket, I was moving around and rushing off to tours too often to make this a convenient option at the time. Furthermore, I didn't want to spend money on breakfast when it was included at the hostels. For lunch each day, I bought a salami and cheese sandwich from the local panaderia in Puerto Madryn because if you brought lunch on the tours, you saved a lot of money (I was learning the ways of the road!). The touristy places were very expensive to eat at, and the salami and cheese was actually delicious and cost $1.00.

One night, I cooked myself breakfast for dinner at the hostel—I purchased two eggs, an avocado, a tomato, and a potato for a total of $3.00 at the local supermarket. Sticking to my budget, I purchased an apple, an orange, and two bananas for my next bus ride, even though I knew I would eat the many alfajores that were offered as well. Sweets were truly becoming my downfall . . . panaderias are a dime a dozen in Argentina, and the baked goods are amazing. Artisanal ice cream could be found everywhere as well. I simply could not resist.

Anyway, back to Day Three. Frederik and I went for a walk on the beach and got some ice cream. Next, I went on a solo mission to indulge in a seafood dinner. As I was reviewing the menu at a potential restaurant, I coincidentally ran into two Scottish guys I had met on the Peninsula Valdes tour, so we had dinner together and shared some travel stories.

Upon my return to the hostel that evening, the Chinese girl in my room was sobbing in bed while talking to someone on the phone. This was quite awkward (and not the first time I encountered a crying girl on my trip). Since I didn't want to interrupt her phone call, I spoke to her the following day and asked her if she was okay. She told me that she was just sad because she was speaking to her husband. I wondered about their arrangement and what she was doing in a hostel in Patagonia, but I simply shared a sympathetic look with her, gave her a hug, and told her everything would be okay (in Spanish, of course).

On Day Five, I visited Punta Tombo, a penguin colony about two and a half hours away from Puerto Madryn. There were 40,000 Magellanic penguins nesting there, and they had recently laid their eggs in this protected area where they migrate every year. It was fascinating, and the penguins came very close to us as we walked around the glorious landscape. On the way to Punta Tombo, the tour stopped in Puerto Rawson for an optional boat ride to see rare black and white dolphins. Again, I skipped this expensive add-on activity and had a coffee while I caught up on some reading about my next stop.

On my final night in Puerto Madryn, I met Frederik and a few of his German friends at another hostel for a few beers. We shared a lot of laughs and I was really happy that all in all, I had a wonderful experience and introduction to Patagonia in Puerto Madryn. Next, I would head south to the freezing temperatures. It was snowing in my next destination —yikes! I could not wait to see the Perito Moreno glacier, which was one of the must-dos on my rough itinerary.

At this point in my trip, I was really starting to appreciate the things I took for granted at home and realize how I did not need so many of the things I had (new car, my own apartment in the city, expensive clothes, etc.). Experiences were so much more valuable to me and I vowed to save money in the future so that I could have more of these experiences rather than a nicer apartment or car, etc. After bearing witness to so much poverty and misfortune along my travels, I reflected upon how lucky I was to be able to eat several meals a day, to walk, to see, to freely make decisions about my life, etc.

Soon, I was off to El Calafate via my fourth 20-hour bus journey, where I'd have plenty of time to contemplate life further.

16

EL CALAFATE / PERITO MORENO - SOUTHERN PATAGONIA

To travel from Puerto Madryn to El Calafate, I took two busses—one for twenty hours, and the next for five hours. The first bus was over two hours late, so I had a grand ol' time hanging around a crappy bus station for hours. Because of the delay, I had to figure out when the next bus would leave the transfer point and if I would make it to my final destination or have to spend a night at the transfer point. Ahhh, the logistics of it all!

My transfer took place in Rio Gallego, which was the southernmost point I had been to thus far. The bus from Puerto Madryn to Rio Gallego was my fourth long haul and the worst yet. The bus itself was filthy and the bathroom and blankets particularly grossed me out. However, I reminded myself that one cannot have high expectations for bus transport in South America.

Before boarding the bus, I met a middle-aged French woman at the bus station in Puerto Madryn who became clingy with me. This woman was very high maintenance, spoke no Spanish, and was rude to the bag porter when he asked her for a tip, proclaiming brashly, "Can you believe he asked me for a tip?!" I tried my best to ignore her, feigning preoccupation with something else. She complained about the bus delay (among other things) and I simply could not deal with her negative presence. I thought, "Lady, you are taking a bus in Argentina, this is not a luxurious situation," and hoped my seat was not near hers.

Mercifully, my seat was not near hers, but it turned out that she was booked into the same hostel as me, so we ended up sharing a taxi upon arrival in El Calafate. Yes, I was willing to put up with this horrible woman to save a few bucks! You may be thinking, "A middle-aged woman staying in a hostel?" but the fact is that many hostels, especially in this region, were very nice and catered to travelers of all ages.

When we finally arrived in El Calafate, my muscles ached as I stepped onto the pavement. I shook off the slight hangover that was clouding my thoughts. The free malbec was pretty much the only good thing about the 25-hour bus journey I had just endured.

Finally, I had reached El Calafate, a small town in southern Patagonia, and while I was weary from travel, I was excited about the next leg of my journey. As I got in line for passport check, I could feel the customary stares setting upon me. A strawberry-blonde American backpacking solo was quite an unusual sight in those parts. I presented my passport, exchanging niceties with the immigration officer in my newly acquired Spanish. He could barely take his eyes off of me to execute his job (or take the shit-eating grin off his face for that matter), as he proclaimed in his best English, "Wow, Estados Unidos, you come long way!"

Back out on the street, I referred to the map in my hand one last time before setting off. Even though I was well into my sabbatical, my Corporate Type-A personality lived on and I had plans, backup plans, maps, and lists related to each of my destinations. Having studied the map of the town on the bus (albeit in a malbec-induced haze), I confirmed my current location and headed toward what appeared to be a taxi stand.

Of course, the Stage Five Clinger French woman was on my heels, asking me where I was headed. When we determined that we were heading to the same place, I agreed to share a taxi with her and vowed to cut off interaction with her after that point.

The sounds of blasting American pop songs from the bus ride rang in my ears as I registered the chill in the air. It was about forty degrees Fahrenheit and very windy. My fleece and raincoat were sufficient for the time being, but I would have to go on a mission to purchase a hat and gloves. I wished I had packed these things, but was trying to be minimalistic. I mentally noted how to say 'hat' and 'gloves' in Spanish and proceeded.

While waiting for a taxi, I broke out the alfajor I had saved from the ride. As a general rule, I had a stomach of steel and would eat pretty much anything, but I had skipped the mystery meat on this bus ride, and hunger suddenly set in. The sugar from the Argentinian cookie combined with the chill in the air reenergized me, and I arrived at the hostel with a spring in my step.

The accommodations were impressive at first glance. The hostel had a classic ski chalet feel, its wooden A-frame set before a backdrop of the snowcapped Andes. I got right down to business upon check-in, inquiring about tour options for hiking the nearby Perito Moreno glacier (making sure the French lady could not hear me). After reviewing the brochure provided to me by the front desk staff, I selected the short trek over the long trek based on its more reasonable price and the fact that I was not yet accustomed to the cold.

With my trek booked for the following day, I dropped my bags in my assigned co-ed dorm room and set off to the town center to purchase a hat, gloves, dinner, and food for my hiking pack.

The Stage Five Clinger saw me leaving the hostel and asked if she could join me but I said I was planning to walk really, really fast (did I mention she had given me the impression she was lazy?!) because I had to get the circulation going after the 25-hour bus trip. I think she got the hint that I wanted to go out alone, and I didn't really mind because I could not handle spending another moment with her. By that point in my travels, I had definitely learned that it is very important to keep your distance from certain people, especially people like her!

In the quaint town center, I easily found a supermarket and purchased bread, sandwich meat, cheese, mustard, nuts, and fruit for my hiking pack. I also bought chicken, pasta, peppers, and onions to cook for dinner. Along the way, I collected cooking ideas from fellow travelers, and I cooked a dish inspired by some of them, making sure to cook enough to last two nights for both time and money saving purposes. The kitchen in the hostel was very small and cramped, so I was glad I would only be preparing one meal in there.

During my trip to the town center, I also shopped around for a hat and gloves, trying to find a bargain. Ultimately, after hitting ten stores, I spent twenty dollars on my cold weather gear, a steep price considering my budget, but completely unavoidable considering the environment I now found myself in.

I was low on pesos, and had yet to visit an Argentinian ATM. To conserve cash, I paid for my hostel, my next bus ticket, the hat and gloves, and my groceries with a credit card, which meant I got the crappy official exchange rate. I paid for the Perito Moreno glacier tour with cash since it was more expensive and I wanted to take advantage of my 'street rate money' for bigger expenditures. I did not want to go to an ATM and was trying to hold out until I got to Chile.

Back at home base, I prepared my clothing and food for the following day's 7:00 AM departure. At the time, I didn't think it was ridiculous at all that I would be wearing a completely mismatched outfit consisting of a bright pink windbreaker, a brown and cream paisley scarf, and a gray hat and gloves.

As I readied myself for bed, the sounds of my roommate clipping his toenails and the stench of my other roommate's hiking boots irked me a bit, but I had learned to accept and deal with these kinds of things. Nothing some earplugs and a spot of Tiger Balm under the nose couldn't solve. I looked forward to bedtime that night, knowing the next day was going to be simply glorious.

Hours later, a sharp pain awoke me in the night. I wondered if I had imagined it, but then I felt another one—a small stab followed by intense itching on my hip. I jumped out of bed with a start as I knew exactly what was happening —I was having another 'incident.' This was the second time this had happened during my two months on the road thus far and I was horrified.

Considering I couldn't turn the lights on as my two room-mates were sleeping in the other bunk, I rushed out of the room and inspected my hip in the dim light of the hallway. It was official—several large welts had already formed. I rushed to the front desk on the verge of tears and asked to be moved to another room. The attendant working the midnight shift couldn't be bothered and informed me that they had nothing else available.

With barely a glance in my direction, he told me that I could move to the top bunk of the bed I was already in if I desired. Given no other choice, I resigned myself to the top bunk, wrapping the sheet tightly around my body, ready to pounce at any hint of another bite. I failed miserably at trying to get the images of swarming bed bugs out of my head. Needless to say, it was a sleepless night as I laid awake dreading further savagery.

At the first hint of daylight, I got up to inspect my body—the attack was worse than I anticipated. Not only did I have several bites on my hips, back, and neck, I was clearly having an allergic reaction as the bites were very swollen.

The morning front desk staffer was just as disinterested as the midnight shifter, simply handing over a tube of itch cream and getting on with their paperwork. I thought, "Ugh!!! This must happen quite often here if they have tubes of itch cream handy behind the counter!" Disgusted, I demanded that my bag and clothes be laundered in very hot water (sadly, I knew the drill) while I was off hiking and that my reservation for the evening be cancelled.

A few minutes later as I dressed in the bathroom, I carefully inspected each and every piece of clothing for bed bugs before putting them on. Next, I inspected my boots and hiking pack fastidiously. I felt like there was no way I could handle yet another 'incident' after this one. My shuttle arrived promptly at 7:00 AM and I climbed in, my mood remarkably different from what I had envisioned the night before. I feigned excitement and a pleasant disposition as I introduced myself to the others in the shuttle. Little did they know, I was screaming inside, both out of frustration and physical pain.

Fortunately, the cold started to numb some of the pain and itch and I was able to turn my focus to my fellow travelers and the breathtaking views as we approached the glacier. Upon arrival, we met our guide under snowy skies, donned boot spikes, and hiked through infinite brilliant hues of blue ice that day. I was in awe, the sheer beauty of my surroundings taking my mind off of my ailment for the time being. The whiskey served over freshly chipped glacier ice at the end of the trek further eased my physical and mental pain.

The tour group gathered for lunch at the end of the hike, and I took the opportunity to visit the ladies' room and tend to my wounds. I pulled the tube of itch cream out of my backpack and applied it liberally to the welts, silently wincing so the women in the other bathroom stalls wouldn't know what I was dealing with. The bites were more swollen than ever, having been irritated by my clothing rubbing against them throughout the day. I felt angry and embarrassed even though it had nothing to do with my personal hygiene. I thought bad-temperedly, "How can this be happening to me when I am in such a beautiful place? What did I do to deserve this? Why me???"

As new tears started to well up, I stopped myself. "Knock it off!" I told myself. "Don't let this ruin such an amazing experience. It is not a big deal in the grand scheme of things. It will pass and one day you will laugh about it." After the pep talk with myself, I soldiered on, making the best of the situation. I wanted to take it all in as there was a high likelihood that I would never make it down to this part of the world again.

Toward the beginning of the tour that day, I met a nice Danish girl who was dealing with some travel issues of her own, albeit of a different kind. Her credit card was not working, she was out of cash, and she couldn't pay her hostel bill, among other things. We buddied up for the day and had fun while we put our issues aside for a while. She wrote down her contact information for me, but when I tried to read it later that evening, I could not read her last name. Therefore, I couldn't find her on Facebook to message her about meeting up for a drink as we had discussed.

Hace freaking frío (It was freaking cold out) anyway so I

just stayed at my new hostel and went to bed early, hoping to wake up in a better state of mind after the incident. I was pretty exhausted after sorting out my bag situation, painstakingly inspecting my laundry, and moving to a new hostel after the hike that day.

On the plus side, I was proud that my big backpack was so lightweight at that point that I could carry it with one arm and it didn't kill me to lift it and walk distances with it. I was getting pretty good at the whole minimizing thing (although I did miss having a wardrobe that consisted of more than ten items)!

I spent that final evening in El Calafate in a hole in the wall hostel that the 'classy' hostel had arranged for me. This hole in the wall did not have bed bugs. After I Facetimed with a friend in the common area that night, another hostel guest approached me as she had overheard my bed bug story. She was a nurse and offered to take a look at my bites. She gasped when I showed her, and told me that I was definitely having an allergic reaction. This very kind nurse made me feel better by relaying an old bed bug story of her own, and recommended taking an antihistamine.

The following day, I awoke early to prepare my belongings and board yet another bus. This one was headed to El Chalten, a magical village home to the famous Cerro Torre and Fitz Roy mountains, about three hours away. As sheer luck would have it, I picked a great seat—from my window seat on the left-hand side of the bus, I took in the extraordinary sight of the sun setting over the jagged, snowcapped peaks of the Andes. I felt at peace in this moment, knowing the universe was giving me a gift—the courage to keep going and not give up because of little hiccups along the way.

As I usually did when moving from place to place, I thought about both what I was grateful for and what I missed about home. I was grateful for the opportunity to be traveling to these beautiful places. I was grateful that I had family and friends at home that cared about my wellbeing. I was grateful that I still had lots of time left in my trip.

I missed things from home, though. Things like coming home to my own space and leaving things in normal places instead of living out of a bag. Things like going to bed without the ever-present fear of being attacked by bed bugs. Things like not having to worry about where I would sleep next, how I would get there, and when I would find the time to figure all of that out. Things like having a fridge full of healthy food and not having to live off of white bread, dulce de leche, cornflakes, and ham. Things like sharing a good laugh over an inside joke with friends.

On days like those after the 'incidents,' I sometimes felt like, "F this!!!!!" but then I would go to a place like the Perito Moreno glacier and realize why I put up with the nonsense— because it was life changing.

17

EL CHALTEN - A MAGICAL VILLAGE IN SOUTHERN PATAGONIA

As I alluded to, the bus ride from El Calafate to El Chalten was remarkable, not only due to the unreal scenery, but also because I met some really nice people at the bus station to sit with for the ride.

It was easy to fall in love with El Chalten—a tiny little town in a valley of the Andes with the most amazing vistas you could ever imagine. The town consists solely of hostels, B&Bs, tiny restaurants, bakeries, and mountain gear shops. All of the activity in the town revolves around hiking—if people are not actually hiking, they are looking at maps and exchanging hiking tips in the hostels and cafés. I had the best luck possible with the weather, getting in three sunny, blue sky days in a row, which is extremely rare in those parts. Many people travel there and don't end up seeing Cerro Torre or Fitz Roy due to cloud cover and bad weather. I was able to experience amazing views of both.

Many new friends and acquaintances had advised me to bring food from El Calafate, as El Chalten is very expensive. I brought pasta, tomatoes, onions, sauce, apples, nuts, and bananas. That was about as much as I could handle carrying in addition to my normal load. Upon arriving at the hostel in El Chalten around 10:00 PM, I spoke with a woman named Cecilia who served as the guide there.

Cecilia showed me some different hikes I could do in the area, filling me in on important details like hike durations and difficulty levels. She was a really awesome 'ski bum' type of lady, full of exuberance and great tips, clearly passionate about her role. The 'easy' hike she recommended was a 6-hour trek to Laguna Torre, from which point you can see the toothy peak of Cerro Torre in the distance. I opted to do this hike the next day so that I could ease my body into things (I was not exactly a picture of health at that time!). After getting that hike under my belt, I would tackle the more difficult one she recommended.

The morning after my arrival, I set out on my own, as I wanted a solo day in the mountains and frankly didn't feel like waiting around for some other characters that were planning to go that day. Undertaking this particular hike on my own was a safe endeavor considering the trail was a very well-travelled one and I would be doing it during daylight hours. The hike was absolutely glorious, and I kept saying to myself, "Wow, wow, wowwwww . . . I can't believe I am here."

Upon reaching Laguna Torre at the summit, I stopped for a rest and to take in the intensely blue lake and soaring pointy peak of Cerro Torre. As I sat on a rock relaxing, I met a very nice Dutch couple. They were hilarious—while they appeared to be in their sixties, they were smoking cigarettes at the summit after a tough hike! I hiked part of the way down with them as we chatted about our respective trips. They had hired a guide, so I was able to capitalize on that, gaining some free knowledge on the local flora and fauna.

Contrary to Cecilia's description, I certainly wouldn't have categorized the hike as 'easy'—I ended up with several blisters on my feet, but this was partly attributable to my boots. My good old trusty hiking boots had let me down, and I ultimately left them behind in El Chalten. One cannot be schlepping around a heavy pair of blister-causing boots on such a trip. I assured myself that Patagonia was a nice resting place for them, and left them on a shelf in the common area of the hostel in case anyone could get some use out of them. Renting gear was typical in this area, so this was not a far-fetched thought.

Considering the state of my feet after Day One, I was planning to take Day Two off and do the more serious, 9-hour Fitz Roy hike on Day Three. However, Cecilia, the trusty guide, told me I HAD to do the Fitz Roy hike on Day Two because of the very rare amazing weather. She informed me that there was a 5-hour option, where I could turn off at a certain point while still getting some great views, if my feet were killing me. Cecilia advised me to hike in my sneakers due to my boot issues and the fact that all of the rental shops were closed (you could rent all sorts of hiking gear, including boots, around town).

Needless to say, I sucked it up and went for it, and it was totally worth it. I didn't even bag out at the 5-hour point, and completed the whole thing with a great group of people that I met. It was so beautiful I can't even begin to describe it. Magical is the best word I can think of to illustrate the overall experience. Not only was the backdrop utterly magnificent, but the company was exceptional, and I spoke Spanish all day.

My hiking partners included a pretty, blonde, bookish woman from Ukraine (specifically Moldova), a fairly clean-cut guy from Ireland, and a long-haired guy from Uruguay wearing a T-shirt that said 'Cannabis.' We all had lots of hilarious Spanglish moments and some really interesting conversation during our nine hours together in the mountains.

I particularly bonded with Eduardo, the Uruguayan guy rocking the weed T-shirt. Eduardo knew some basic English and I was getting 'decent' at communicating in Spanish (read: I could get my point across, albeit in a laughable fashion at times). We described our lives back home to one another—what we did for work, what we did for fun, what brought us to these parts.

During our conversation, we would help each other learn words that we didn't know in each other's native language. The conversation flowed easily and the hours flew by. The two of us ended up lagging a bit behind the rest of the crew which could've been because we couldn't stop talking or maybe because we weren't as physically fit as the others.

Regardless, at one point, when I thought the hike couldn't get any more glorious, we came across a young couple, startling them as the they looked guiltily at us. I caught a whiff of the weed at that point as Eduardo asked, "Fumas marijuana?" ("Are you smoking marijuana?"). They had noticed my friend's shirt by this point and knew he was a comrade so they said yes and offered us some. We accepted and the four of us smoked the joint that they had brought along. After hiking together as a foursome for a bit, we parted ways—they were younger and more fit so steamed on ahead.

Eduardo and I, high as kites high in the Andes, continued our banter which was augmented by the pot. We came across a fork in the trail with a sign displaying what appeared to be an upcoming rotary. Upon referencing our handheld maps (smart hikers, prepared ahead of time courtesy of Cecilia!), we determined that there were two routes we could take—one of which was much longer than the other.

Neither the sign itself, nor the map, were clear about which way was longer—or maybe the weed was affecting our judgement? We laughed and laughed but also stressed a bit, as we were worn out from hiking for hours and wanted to minimize remaining hiking time at this point in the journey. We had already peaked, literally and figuratively.

Finally, an executive decision was made and we carried on confidently. As we continued along, I achieved a serious milestone, making my first joke in Spanish. It was actually funny and I'll never forget that moment. "Un Chiste!!! Woo hoo!!" I laughed out, slapping my new friend five as he shared in my glory. I only wish I could remember the joke. Again, must have been the weed . . . but what a great bond we created that day!

After the hike that day, my hiking 'team' and I treated ourselves to a nice dinner at a restaurant called El Muro. One of my roommates, Jean, ex-CFO of a Swiss train company that had quit his job to travel the world, also joined us. The restaurant we dined at received rave reviews in my Lonely Planet guide, and it lived up to those reviews that night. We all shared the mixed parilla, which consisted of a massive quantity of different meats. Cordero (lamb) is the typical meat in Patagonia and it tastes especially delicious after nine hours of hiking. In addition to the meats, we also had our fill of veggies and of course, indulged in some locally brewed beers. It was quite simply, lovely.

On Day Three in El Chalten, I rested and got some important things accomplished, like booking my next hostel, figuring out how to get to and from the airports that would be involved, drinking coffees, and eating baked goods. Once evening rolled around, I went for beers with my friends at a local hippie bar called Mito's. It was an adorable little establishment, with colorful décor, quirky furniture, and a cozy loft area where we hung out. After our little happy hour, we went out for pizzas, and then my friends all left on a bus headed north for Bariloche.

Day Four was my final day in the lovely little mountain town. To soak it all up one more time, I rented a mountain bike and cycled to a waterfall. It was an absolutely brilliant, albeit very windy, ride with the stunning backdrop I was starting to take for granted—the snowcapped Andes.

As I reflected during my ride, I had but one small regret from my time in El Chalten. I was invited to go camping in the mountains by a new, extremely handsome Dutch acquaintance not long after I had arrived and I did not take him up on this offer. I declined for a few reasons: 1. I thought that it might be dangerous considering I was unfamiliar with this person and the area, 2. I felt too unprepared in terms of gear. In hindsight, I realized how easy it was to make a split-second decision to camp, rent all the gear you need, and just go for it.

During one of my hikes, I ran into this guy and a few others he was camping with and their setup looked amazing. While I regretted not joining them, my decision to not camp made it possible for me to meet the other friends with whom I had an unforgettable time.

During my final evening in the hostel common area, I met a few American girls that were on a three-week vacation to Patagonia. I have to admit that watching them bicker about where to go and what to do next, etc. made me really appreciate my solo traveling. The beauty of it was that I could do whatever I wanted, whenever I wanted.

It was fairly rare to meet Americans in those parts, but I did meet a few others. Unfortunately, they were folks that I chose to avoid and not be associated with for the most part based on their behavior. These particular people were substantiating the stereotypes that people have of the American traveler—being ignorant, rude, and loud while making zero attempt to speak Spanish. They assumed the world would revolve around their native language and basically caused a scene upon arrival. Just for the record, I love my home country and am a proud American. I simply cannot tolerate loud, ignorant people.

So, where was I headed next? After much contemplation, I decided on my next move and planned to fly to Mendoza from southern Patagonia. This was a divergence from my prospective plan of heading to Torres del Paine National Park in southern Chile next. Originally, I wanted to take the Navimag boat up the Chilean coast after hiking the infamous 'W' in Torres del Paine.

However, I decided against this plan for a few reasons: 1. The weather looked terrible, which meant trekking in Torres del Paine would be miserable. It also meant that the boat may not sail due to inclement weather. If this situation played out, I would be stuck in a place called Puerto Natales, paying for a room and waiting around for the weather to improve—not exactly in my budget. 2. Southern Patagonia is expensive, and I needed to get back up north to help my wallet!

Speaking of my wallet, pulling the trigger on the flight to Mendoza was a bit painful, as it cost $340.00 and was my most expensive transport leg yet. However, I knew that once I was there, bus travel would become easier again. The flight was at a very inconvenient time: 2:00 AM departure from El Calafate. The airport transfer shuttle from the hostel would get me there way too early, but was really the only option and there would be plenty of other people in the same boat. The alternative to flying was forty hours of bus travel, and I could not handle being on a bus for that long. I had taken enough busses for the time being and knew there were more in my future so I chose to treat myself to a flight. I was looking forward to wine, cheese, and olives galore in Mendoza!

18

MENDOZA - LAND OF THE WORLD'S
BEST MALBEC

I t was a smooth trip to Mendoza by air, preceded by an expected long wait at the airport. I ran into someone I recognized from my hostel in Buenos Aires at the airport, so we hung out for a bit. This was convenient, as the airport in southern Patagonia does not have any bar or restaurant scene where you can kill a few hours. Your options basically include lying down on the ground for a nap or reading a book.

When I arrived at the hostel in Mendoza, I met some new pals right away. We were simultaneously checking in and inquiring about local wine tours, so got to chatting. My new crew included three nice English folks and an American girl. The English group included a girl about my age, Emma, her boyfriend, Gareth, and her brother, Paul. They were all traveling together for a few months and this was one of their last stops. The American girl, Jessica, was on a shorter solo trip. I ended up spending most of my time with these folks while in Mendoza.

On Day One, we wasted no time and rented bikes in the Maipu region with a few other people from the hostel. We cycled to three wineries, taking tours, learning about the environment and grapes, and tasting lots of wine. I quickly and easily learned that the malbec is absolutely divine in this part of the world. It shouldn't come as a surprise that we got quite drunk—in fact, I fell off my bike just before we were about to return them as I was looking around distractedly at the beautiful scenery! No serious injuries ensued—just a minor scrape on my hand and a bruise on my leg. After our day of biking around the vineyards, we cooked a great meal on the hostel's BBQ—grilled sausages, peppers, and asparagus.

On Day Two, my new crew and I went to the Cacheuta thermal spas, an amazing place nestled in a valley of the Andes on the border of Argentina and Chile. This outing was an organized day trip that we signed up for and it included transport, admission to the natural hot springs, and a massive, high quality buffet lunch. Of course, we ordered a few bottles of malbec with lunch, which cost us next to nothing.

In addition to partaking in the recommended circuit of hot and cool baths, we took mud baths, lounged in the sauna, and I even splurged on a $15.00 massage. The white towels and robes, white lounge chairs perched on green grass, and glimmering pools made for an idyllic setting among the towering mountains. It was an incredibly relaxing day and I felt spoiled for the first time in a while, sauntering around in my white robe, glass of malbec in hand, surrounded yet again by the grand Andes. As I'm writing this years later, I still can't get over how I executed this entire six-month trip for less than most people spend on a week or two in Europe!

Because we couldn't get enough of the local wine and had heard wondrous things about the Lujan region, my new friends and I rented bikes in that region on Day Three. We biked to several vineyards, participating in each of the standard tastings and also buying a few glasses of the high-end stuff to share. As we rode through Lujan, beautiful parks and flowering trees abounded. We paused in one of many lovely parks and took a little siesta in between tastings. In every direction, glorious vineyards with magnificent flowers and lush landscapes revealed themselves.

I wished I could take a little piece of this place home with me. On that note, I wanted to ship some wine home for friends and family, but the cost of shipping was outrageous—the minimum shipping cost was $196.00 so I passed on that! Toward the end of our bike tour in Lujan, we made a drunken pitstop at a quaint shop that specialized in olive oil, liqueur, absinthe, and chocolate. More tasting of local products ensued. As we went to leave this place, Paul's handlebar simply fell right off his bike! You can imagine the amusement we all got out of this after sipping malbec and absinthe all day. As we all laughed uncontrollably, he rode without a handlebar to our final stop of the day, a restaurant where we indulged in massive burgers.

Wasting no time, the crew and I made the not-so-logical decision to walk to a viewpoint overlooking the city in 90+ degree heat with wine hangovers on Day Four in Mendoza. We were all dying by the time we reached the summit and ultimately took a taxi home! We managed to have a nice lunch in a park along on our travels, however, which was the most productive thing that happened that day.

On my final day in Mendoza, I ventured off to the bus station to get a ticket to Santiago, Chile, which would be my next stop. The bus ride from Mendoza to Santiago promised to be a very scenic/death-defying ride through the Andes. After purchasing my ticket, I walked to City Hall to get one last tourist attraction in, as you can view the city and mountains from a terrace on the seventh floor there. This was pretty, but a bit underwhelming. I moved on to a nice café where I of course indulged my new espresso habit.

On the way back to home base, I stopped into a super-market and bought some food for my upcoming bus trip. Finally, I went out to meet a friend that I had originally met in Buenos Aires for a quick museum visit, dinner, and vino. I was really packing it in!

Mendoza was lovely, and I most certainly developed a new fondness for malbec! Next up, I planned to spend a couple of nights in a hostel in Santiago and then possibly stay at a family friend's condo in that area. I wasn't sure how long I would stay in the Santiago area, but I knew my next stop after that would be San Pedro de Atacama in the Atacama Desert. Then I would make my way to Bolivia, visiting the Uyuni Salt Flats, La Paz, and Sucre.

19

SANTIAGO & VALPARAISO, CHILE

The bus ride from Mendoza to Santiago was CRAZY! If you ever get the chance, you should take it. The route traverses the Andes and the dramatic scenery includes a ribbon-like road winding through multi-hued, snow-capped mountains. The mineral-induced, layered coloring of the mountains is a true natural marvel. I tried to secure the upstairs front window seat in the bus, but booked my ticket a few minutes too late which was a bummer. I was getting more laid back about booking things in advance and had booked the bus ticket to Santiago just one day in advance.

This bus ride was actually a bit scary, as there were countless hairpin turns, and the driver of our massive bus had no problem passing tractor trailers on the narrow, windy, mountain roads. At one point, I even witnessed the aftermath of a pretty terrible head-on collision between two tractor trailers. One truck was on its side about to fall off the mountain road into a deep valley, and the other was on its side on fire.

While the trip was supposed to take seven hours, including an allowance for an hour at the border, it took us eight hours, as a Chilean lady was smuggling thirty massive bottles of olive oil, twenty massive bags of laundry detergent, and ten cartons of cigarettes. Unfortunately, all of the passengers in the bus had to wait around while the customs officials dealt with her.

I was exhausted upon arrival in Santiago, so I just had dinner near the hostel and called it a night quite early. There were five Irish guys in my room who were the sloppiest people I had encountered yet on the trip. They went to a concert on my first night in the hostel and came back very drunk, so in the morning, the room smelled glorious. These guys were very nice people, but fortunately, they checked out after that first night.

Night Two in the hostel was free pasta and wine night and I obviously planned to capitalize on this. As some folks gathered before dinner, a guy from New Zealand bought a twelve-pack and offered everyone beer, which promoted a very social atmosphere.

I did some power sightseeing in Santiago, discovering wonderful markets and hidden gems of eateries through a free walking tour I took. Previously, I was 'anti-walking tour,' but when someone convinced me to tag along on one at one point, I was sold and in fact, looked for them as I traveled from place to place thereafter.

The walking tour took us through several markets, which are always a feast for the senses. In Santiago's markets, pyramids of fruits and vegetables lined the aisles. I spotted the most massive calamari I had ever seen, vendors napping in their stalls, and even an old man with a rainbow-colored spinning top hat.

I had lunch at Central Market, a place where most 'normal' Americans would not eat—it was recommended by a local on the walking tour, though, and I was all about mingling with the locals and experiencing the real deal. I was advised to eat the cazuela, a traditional soup, and boy, did it deliver. I have yet to find one in America that comes close to the one I had in the bowels of that market!

The walking tour also took us through the cementarios of Santiago. These are cemeteries with above-ground graves. This part of the tour was powerful and fascinating. The grave of a three-year-old, decadently adorned with stuffed animals and bright decorations, brought me to tears.

While I was only in Santiago for a few days, I was also able to take in the Bellas Artes Museum and Saint Lucia Park. With San Cristobal overlooking the city from a hilltop, there was a constant feeling of the presence of God. I walked and I walked and I walked. This was a good thing, because I was eating like a total pig—things like French fries topped with meat and gravy, endless sweets, and more!

One day as I was walking, I saw a sign that said 'Brighton'—it was a reminder of home that elicited a twang of pain and longing that surprised me. Brighton is the neighborhood in Boston where I lived before giving it all up to travel, so it was a coincidence to see a sign with that name in the middle of Santiago.

Interestingly enough, I had received an offer from my uncle's partner to stay in his condo in the Santiago area if I so desired. While this man lived in Boston, he kept the condo in his hometown of Santiago for vacation purposes. An aunt passed along the offer through Facebook when she noticed where I was in my trip.

So, after two nights in the hostel, I navigated my way to his place on the metro with all of my baggage during rush hour. The metro situation coupled with finding the actual condo was a bit complex, but I eventually arrived at my destination, located in a very local neighborhood.

The condo was nicely appointed and a friend of the family met me upon my arrival to let me in. I enjoyed a night of relaxation, giving myself a manicure and pedicure and catching up on some reading. However, the place was a bit off the beaten path for me and did not have WiFi, so I only spent one night. At that point in my trip, WiFi was essential to figuring out my next move and the logistics that would go along with it.

Admittedly, I was suffering from a bit of exhaustion at that point—I was moving constantly and having to figure out all sorts of things including modes of transport, places to stay, and immigration requirements. WiFi was totally necessary for this research, so I had to get back to a place that provided it.

From the condo, I navigated back to central Santiago, where I met a very cool American girl, Laura, in the hostel. I traveled to Valparaiso with her and an English girl that we met. Valparaiso is a very quaint, seaside town near Santiago known for its art. Vividly colored paint and creative graffiti covers every surface, whether it's a building, a wall, or a set of stairs.

As I mentioned, I had become fond of free walking tours, so Laura and I took the walking tour of Valparaiso on Day One to become acquainted with the place. That evening, we went out with some college students that were Laura's friends of friends, which turned out to be a fun night of mojito and pisco sour drinking. The rest of the time in Valparaiso involved sightseeing and eating. One of the highlights was a visit to Pablo Neruda's house (now a museum). After a few short days, I hustled back to Santiago to prepare for the next leg of my journey.

New countries meant new exchange rates and the need to plan accordingly for disposal and acquisition of local currency. I foolishly ended up with Argentinian pesos upon arrival to Chile and had to take a hit at the cambio shop, so planning for this type of thing was added to my agenda going forward. It was difficult to plan how much currency I would need—if I didn't take out enough, I would need to visit the ATM more frequently and pay additional ATM fees. If I took out too much, I would get screwed at the cambio shop when I left the country.

So . . . the constant moving, researching, money changing, meal planning, struggling to keep electronics charged in places with one outlet that barely works, etc. made for an exhausting few weeks. This was exacerbated by the very sketchy or completely absent WiFi.

I was not able to find the time to research San Pedro or the Bolivian Salt Flats (a.k.a. Salar de Uyuni or Uyuni Salt Flats), which would be my next two stops. I felt stressed, as I heard that the Chile to Bolivia border crossing could be difficult. Putting my anxieties aside for the time-being, I assured myself that I would figure it all out upon arrival in San Pedro, in northern Chile. Some other travelers had told me that it was very expensive in San Pedro so I didn't want to stay too long, but I would stay as long as I needed to in order to figure out my next steps.

I was looking forward to getting to Sucre, Bolivia eventually because I planned to settle down there for a bit and relax. I was also really looking forward to experiencing the Uyuni Salt Flats, where I would be doing a three or four-day tour. Word on the street was that you don't want to be in a 4x4 vehicle for three days with six people you don't like, so I hoped to find a cool group of people while I was in San Pedro with whom to do the multi-day tour.

Ready to depart Santiago, I got my bus ticket and got ready for my next 24-hour bus ride.

20

SAN PEDRO DE ATACAMA

My next stop was San Pedro de Atacama, which is in the Atacama Desert in the northern part of Chile (the most arid desert in the world). This place is considered the entryway into the Uyuni Salt Flats and is home to excursion and souvenir shops, and not much else.

For the 24-hour bus ride, I booked the semi-cama seat as it was half the price of the cama seat. However, the semi-cama seat was 'sin servicio' which translates literally to 'without service,' meaning it did not include food or drink. It also meant that the seat doesn't recline fully. This was okay with me, though, as I had scored a front seat on the second level of the bus which was prime real estate in terms of viewing perspective.

I had to prepare some food to bring, so I hustled to get some sandwich materials and crackers when I returned from Valparaiso to Santiago. I made a delicious sandwich worth looking forward to, and then of course, forgot the sandwich in the hostel fridge when I left. To make matters worse on the day of my departure, the hostel wasn't serving breakfast because the staff was late, so I had to go to the bus station via metro with all of my bags during rush hour, eat a bus station breakfast, and board a crappy bus for twenty-four hours. Can you tell I was getting frustrated with some of the travel snafus?! Fortunately, I was able to laugh about these things (after the fact, of course) and keep the big picture in mind.

I thought things were looking up when I saw an empanada stand at the first stop that the bus made. I hurried over and tried to buy an empanada, but the vendor didn't have enough change so I couldn't buy it. All of the other hot food vendors at this pitstop were closed, so I purchased several packages of generic Oreos, which I ate for breakfast, lunch, and dinner.

A disgusting, fat man reeking of booze boarded the bus and sat next to me for the next few hours. I grumpily ate my Oreos and pretended to sleep so that I wouldn't have to talk to him. Luckily, he was transferred to a different bus when we blew a tire in the middle of the desert (I'll get to this). I was totally exhausted at that point, which I'm sure can be gleaned through my negative tone. I was able to sleep for about ten hours on the bus and I watched a few movies, so it could've been worse. Rest was illusory and I looked forward to more of it. However, my exhaustion was very different from that I used to experience back home. It was not work stress that was exhausting me which made it more bearable in a strange way.

As I indulged in some much-needed sleep, I was awoken by a bang and the veering of the bus. The back right tire had blown out as we traveled through the middle of the desert. It would take hours before anyone could reach us with a spare. Passengers could either sit around for what ended up being two hours either inside the bus or outside in the desert. I chose to hang outside considering the already extremely long bus ride in a non-reclining seat was now growing longer.

Outside, I met two French guys that appeared to be about my age, Michel and Alexandre, who were also headed to the Bolivian Salt Flats via San Pedro de Atacama. We chatted and joked around as we waited for the mechanic to arrive. Both guys were attractive but in totally different ways. Michel did most of the talking, as he was fluent in English due to a high school exchange stint in Iowa. Alexandre could speak very little English. It was adorable when he tried, though!

With Alexandre's basic English and Spanish, we could communicate on some level, but anything complex had to go through Michel. Alexandre had a completely different tone when he was speaking rapid fire French to Michel and I was sad that I couldn't communicate with him easily in words. "Soy abogado!" ("I am a lawyer!"), proclaimed Alexandre as we swapped background stories in the desert. He enunciated each syllable so strongly and Michel and I laughed as Michel explained in English that they were lawyers on sabbatical for a year together. He told me that in France, you can take a year off and be guaranteed to get your job back upon your return.

Michel was clearly very smart, and his perfectly spoken English would've almost led me to mistake him for an American if he didn't have a French accent. He looked the part of a smart French lawyer, with some premature hair loss and a serious look on his face when he was thinking. I would soon learn, however, that he was never serious, and in fact, quite the opposite! Alexandre looked more like an international man of leisure, effortlessly handsome with olive skin and perfectly coiffed brown hair.

Once the tire was changed, we all went back to our seats, agreeing to meet up in San Pedro once we arrived. Due to my fatigue, I wanted to find accommodation quickly when we got to the town. My new French buddies were planning to pound the pavement to make some comparisons and look for a deal, so we split up at my hostel with a promise of a visit later that evening.

When they visited that night, they invited me to join them on a 32-kilometer bike ride through the desert to Valle de la Luna. I agreed and we set off the next day to this very unique, moon-like place. During our ride, we got to know one another, and I was pleased to discover that these guys had a great sense of humor—in fact, they were hilarious.

Unfortunately, on the bike ride home from Valle de la Luna, I became so dehydrated and got a skull-crushing headache. Because of this, the journey 'home' on the bike seemed like it would never end. When I finally did arrive home, I was welcomed by a cramped dorm room, a cat laying in my bed, and an empty soap dispenser in the shared bathroom.

While I don't like to highlight the negative aspects of long-term travel, I believe that it's important to share the reality of it all so you know that it's not all fun and games! My experience in Chile cemented the fact that hostels in this country were worse than those in Argentina. On a positive note, one of my roommates, Josephine from Switzerland, turned out to be a lovely woman who I would maintain a long-term relationship with and meet again during my travels.

Josephine was a tall, slender brunette who sacrificed nothing in terms of style while traveling. Her long brown hair always looked great and you would never guess that she was backpacking based on the stylish clothes she wore. Josephine was dating someone in Chile and had been in San Pedro for some time. However, she planned to continue her travels, so we made sure to exchange information so that we could meet again if our paths crossed.

Continuing on that positive note, I was slated to leave for a three-day trip through the Uyuni Salt Flats in Bolivia. Lucky for me, I had made fast friends with Michel and Alexandre, so we booked the trip together. As I mentioned, this trip involves spending a great deal of time in a 4x4 vehicle with six people (seven including the driver) over the course of three days so it is recommended to go with people whose company you enjoy. The 'French guys,' as I began to fondly refer to them as, were great company—they were hilarious, fun to be with, and smart. The three other tourists in our jeep would be a surprise and we hoped for a pleasant one!

Booking this sub-trip was a complicated project in itself, as there were several vendors in town and it was the norm to bargain with them to find the best quality at the best price. Challenges arose with communication and receiving confir-mations because phone service and WiFi were unreliable and vendors were frequently out of the office. Fellow travelers were great resources, and everyone was always exchanging stories about which companies were best, but it was still difficult to choose one.

Ultimately, we settled on an outfit called Estrella del Sur, and we got a deal because we booked as a group of three. The French guys were great at bargaining and got the best deals on lodging and excursions. I was glad to have them on my side while booking this excursion—their patience was a lot greater than mine.

We were set to depart early one morning at 7:30 AM. I was anticipating a very interesting adventure . . . the land-scapes were supposed to be some of the most spectacular in the world. The nights were supposed to be quite cold and the accommodations were rumored to be questionable. However, word on the street was that this would be an experience of a lifetime.

As always, I had to consider my next moves so that I knew what to do when the journey ended in Uyuni, Bolivia. Tentatively, I planned to spend one night in Uyuni at the end of the three-day tour, then get on a bus to Sucre, Bolivia. At that point, it was looking like I would be spending Thanksgiving in Sucre. I planned to settle there for a couple weeks, relax, and brush up on my Spanish—Sucre was known for its cheap, private Spanish lessons. I was super excited for the trip, but anxious about the Bolivian border crossing which was reputed as more complex than others!

Before leaving San Pedro, I purchased myself a copper ring during a stroll through the local market. Chile is a major copper exporter and copper mining is a key industry in northern Chile. Beautiful copper wares could be found in the local markets for short money, so I decided to treat myself to a memento. When I saw a ring I wanted, I tried it on, but it was too big. The guy manning the shop told me he would make it smaller for me, so while I poked around for a bit, he custom-fitted my intricate $10.00 copper ring, which I still cherish to this day.

During this shopping trip, I also purchased a bracelet to add to my wrist to represent the country of Chile. Many travelers I had met wore a collection of bracelets from the different places they had visited. I liked this idea and had a head start with the bracelet Gianfranco had given me in Argentina, so I picked up a cute woven bracelet that resembled the friendship bracelets from my middle school days.

21

EPIC ADVENTURE IN THE BOLIVIAN SALT FLATS

The adventure into the Uyuni Salt Flats (the largest salt flats in the world) was everything I had dreamed of and much, much more! The night before departure, the French guys came to my hostel to hang out with Josephine and I for one last hurrah in San Pedro. We planned to take it easy, as you are not supposed to drink more than one glass of wine prior to the ascent to the salt flats, but our evening quickly turned into a hostel dance party.

Bright and early the next day, the vehicle that I would spend much of the next three days in picked me up at the hostel. It was an old and not very well-maintained Lexus LX450. I saw that there were three other passengers so far and the French guys were not among them.

As I climbed into the third row of seats, I introduced myself to the three women—Sofia from Germany, Zoe from the Netherlands, and Celina from Spain. The driver, Fernando, was a Bolivian who appeared to be no more than sixteen years old. I told the women that I knew the final two passengers that we would be picking up and that they were two fun French guys from Paris.

Once we were all packed in and on the road, we chatted and got to know one another. Sofia and Zoe were about the same age as me, and Celina was about ten or so years older. Sofia and Zoe had met a few weeks back in Argentina and had been traveling together for a bit. They admitted to being hungover and we all laughed as Michel, Alexandre, and I made the same confession.

Sofia was classically beautiful so it came as no surprise that she made her living as an actress back home. She had long straight dirty blonde hair and unlike most American actresses that are too skinny, Sofia had a great, healthy body. Her intelligence was apparent as she spoke in a very direct way in near perfect English. Sofia and I would get to know one another very well in the coming weeks.

Zoe gave off a girl next door tomboy vibe but I would soon learn that she was also a total flirt. Tall and lean, with striking eyes and a mischievous smile, she was naturally pretty without makeup. Back home, she was a special education teacher. These two women would become very close friends of mine. From the start, they gave off positive vibes only and it was clear that they were no bullshit, confident, beautiful, hilarious women who empowered others to be their best.

I learned more about the French guys as well. Michel joked about how Alexandre was from the rich part of Paris and how he himself lived in the slums. While these guys were heterosexual, their bromance was enviable—they rarely argued and would hug it out frequently. Even though they were on the road together for months already and had several months to go, they could still be together every moment, constantly speaking to one another in their sidebar French conversations.

We all taught Alexandre phrases in English and had him repeat after us. As I mentioned, he enunciated everything so intensely and we would all laugh (fortunately, he was a good sport and we were laughing with him and not at him). It was amazing how much communication we accomplished through our eyes and gestures and piecing three languages together!

Celina was very quiet, but friendly. She only spoke Spanish, and the rest of us predominantly communicated in English, so it was tough for her to keep up with everything. I translated everything I could. Celina suffered from the altitude worse than any of us, so we usually reserved the front seat for her and she sat there quietly with her eyes closed to ward off the headaches. Celina was very fit for her age, an avid hiker and biker. She was a true saint for putting up with the rest of us during the trip!

As a group, we discussed the logistics of the border crossing and the fact that we were about to ascend to some serious altitude. Fernando, our timid, boyish driver, told us he had some coca leaves that we could chew on to help us cope with the altitude.

Coca leaves are a major crop in the Andes and are the source of cocaine. While chewing them in their raw form can serve as a stimulant, it is not at all equivalent to doing cocaine. The leaves need to go through a process in order to be transformed into cocaine.

Fernando spoke in a sheepish tone, barely making eye contact at first. Of course, by the end of the trip, we had him smiling and laughing with us.

Upon arrival to the Bolivian border and immigration office, we all looked at each other incredulously and burst out laughing. The office was literally a shack in the middle of nowhere . . . very official! However, I was still apprehensive about the border crossing. My fears turned out to be totally unfounded, as the officials were very kind and did not give me any problems with my documentation. There was even a bonus—the visa cost me $60.00 as opposed to the expected $135.00. My trusty website, travel.state.gov, needed to update their information!

The next three days were nothing short of epic. We drove for hours to our first stop, a very shabby hostel in the middle of nowhere with no showers or heat. During the drive, our altitude steadily increased and the temperature steadily dropped. Michel and Celina became sick from the altitude, experiencing terrible headaches which were only partially relieved by the coca leaves.

Upon arrival to the hostel on a very chilly Night One, we were told that there would only be two hours of electricity which meant we had to be sure to charge our electronics during that time. The whole situation at this hostel can only be described as 'innnnnteresting.' My new friends picked up on my overuse of the word 'interesting' and we all started to say it constantly in English, Spanish, and French.

The six of us on the tour shared a cold drab room, where we had to pile on grungy blankets in order to keep warm for the night. There were a few other people staying at this hostel and several of us stood around a woodstove with head lamps on in the center of a bare room drinking smuggled wine that night. It was here that we met a couple of new Swedish friends, Lars and Hans. They were on a separate tour but we would run into them several times along the way.

After imbibing around the woodstove for a bit, we grabbed some blankets and went outside to look at the stars. I can confidently say that this was and will forever be the most brilliant stargazing experience of my life. It must have been the altitude and our proximity to the cosmos—the clear night sky was simply brilliant.

The next day Fernando rushed us into the jeep, becoming impatient with the pace of some of the crew. He started the car with a screwdriver as we all looked on in awe. Fernando spoke very little to no English, but we were able to communicate nonetheless. Fortunately, Celina's native language was Spanish and the rest of us knew enough to get by.

Our unflappable driver let us blast music of our choice and he would blast his own when we didn't have a preference as we bombed through the salt flats. In all reality, it was a very dangerous adventure. We sped through clouds of dust so dense that there was zero visibility, as Michel yelled out, "We're going to die!!!" I had read that death by car accident was not exactly uncommon on the salt flats. The crew and I would scream as we sped through the clouds of dust, half laughing and half fearing for our lives.

We raced around all day, making pit stops to view magnificent, unearthly vistas and check out packs of llamas and flamingos. Somehow, jokes about llamas and flamingos became the norm in our everyday conversations. The altitude must have really been affecting us, as Michel asked us all at one point, "Would you rather have sex with a llama or eat only flamingo for the rest of your life?" We all laughed at the disgusting question and agreed that we could never subsist solely off of flamingo for the rest of our lives. Being in the car all day for several days also meant lots of singalongs and teaching each other words in different languages. A favorite phrase of the group was "Vamos arriba!" and we would yell it out whenever we were going uphill to Fernando's quiet amusement.

No trip to the salt flats would be complete without taking perspective photos, known as 'fotos locos' (crazy photos). These are photos in which some items appear unusually huge while others appear tiny even though they are very close to one another. Because of this, you can create photos in which it looks like someone is holding another person in the palm of their hand or someone is stepping on an entire group of people, etc.

Many folks use props such as toy dinosaurs, as the perspective makes it look like huge dinosaurs are chasing people. Fernando provided us with some little props and we took several fotos locos, which I have hanging in my home to this day. The whole crew, including our trusty driver, climbed on top of the vehicle to capture that special moment in time in a group photo.

Each day along our route, Fernando would set up a buffet on the tailgate of the jeep for lunch and we would share meals while sitting on rocks in the desert. Little desert bunnies would hop by looking for a scrap. The altitude was extreme and was affecting some of us more than others. I was very lucky and only suffered from a little shortness of breath. Poor Michel and Celina were continuing to suffer quite a bit with headaches and nausea. Chewing coca leaves helped us all a bit (and no, they didn't get us high!).

The salt flats, while desert, looked like water. An endless mirage, I suppose. The landscape was primarily a bare, cracked valley with colorful mineral-induced mountains surrounding it. The sunsets were brilliant. One area was inhabited by cacti that appeared very similar to the Saguaro cacti found in the southwest US. We visited sights of abandoned trains and train tracks, taking eerie photos amid the extreme wind that was fairly characteristic of each day.

We spent Night Two in a hostel made entirely of salt (even the beds!). This place was an upgrade to the first night, which was a pleasant surprise. Celina was my roommate during this night. Fernando set up our dinner in the common area where we all congregated and enjoyed a delicious meal and lots of laughs.

As we talked over more smuggled wine, the crew told me that they thought I needed to do something else with my career—that I belonged with people, not sitting behind a desk. I whole-heartedly agreed but had no idea what this something could be considering I had invested so much in the career I already had.

The trip ended in Uyuni, Bolivia, a very sad ramshackle town. We were all disappointed the experience was over, as we had SUCH an amazing time! This part of my trip was by far filled with the most laughter. It was exactly what I needed at a point in my trip where exhaustion was setting in and I was starting to become a little negative. My traveling partners and I created a bond that would last a lifetime and a few of us would go on to travel together for a while afterward. In fact, some of us would celebrate Thanksgiving, Christmas, and the New Year together!

I'd be remiss if I didn't note that, while naturally rich and beautiful, Bolivia is the poorest country in South America and it is very difficult to witness the lives that many people lead there. Children work in the mines at the age of seven years old. People live in very basic shacks with no windows or roofs in many cases. There is rampant poverty and filth in the streets.

It was very humbling to travel through this country. In the spirit of the looming Thanksgiving holiday, I felt really fortunate not only to have the opportunity to travel, but also to have food, shelter, and people back home that loved me.

22

SUCRE, BOLIVIA

Sofia, Zoe, the French guys, and I stayed in Uyuni for one night after the salt flats excursion. We did not want to stay long as the accommodations were questionable at best. The following day, we all boarded a bus bound for Sucre (via Potosi). The 8-hour bus ride from Uyuni to Sucre wasn't as bad as expected. As was the norm during all of my bus rides, the roads were very windy, so we bumped around in our seats quite a bit. The bus was nothing like the 'luxury' ones in Argentina, but I was expecting much worse.

The French guys got off the bus in the mining town of Potosi. The girls and I decided not to visit Potosi, as we thought it would be too disturbing. We had heard that when you tour the mines, you are expected to bring the miners alcohol as gifts because they get very drunk all day while they work. As I've also alluded to, there was word that children as young as seven years old worked in the mines. This was simply too depressing for me to witness, and Sofia and Zoe felt the same way. When we met up with the guys again a few days later, they relayed stories of bringing strong alcohol into the mines and getting drunk with the miners, but claimed they did not see any children.

I was pleasantly surprised upon arrival to Sucre, a cute, colonial city with whitewashed buildings and terracotta rooftops. Like everywhere else in Bolivia, it is surrounded by mountains. Women in traditional Bolivian dress (full skirts and wide-rimmed hats topping long braids) walked along the sidewalks and staffed market stalls. During my time in Sucre, the skyscapes particularly struck me . . . from crazy hail-storms and unusual rings around the moon to extraordinary sunsets.

The girls and I stayed at a hostel that cost about $7.00 each per night. We shared a room that had two sets of bunkbeds and a single bed, and we had the room to ourselves initially. The hostel offered a discount if you signed up to take Spanish lessons there, but their classes were full during the first week. Anxious to get more lessons under my belt, I went to another school for a few days, but took the classes at the hostel the following week. I took private lessons, which were helpful at that point in my Spanish speaking quest.

Since I had almost three months of travel under my belt already, these lessons focused on more complex conversation in addition to past and future tenses. My teacher, a Bolivian guy in his twenties, told me that my main issue was shyness. He suggested that I put myself out there more and just prac-tice because that was all I really needed at that point. I promised that I would.

Everything was pretty cheap in Bolivia, from food to accommodation. You could get a huge dinner with drinks for less than $7.00 at a reputable place and if you ate in the market, you could eat a big lunch for $2.00. Spanish classes were also plentiful and cheap, making Sucre a popular desti-nation for those wanting to learn or improve their Spanish.

Taking advantage of the low prices, I even purchased a

cheap watch in Bolivia because the one I had started out with had broken. My new timepiece was a sporty black plastic one with a purple face, which enhanced my already ridiculous, mismatched outfits.

Zoe, Sofia, and I had become fast friends and were having lots of fun and endless laughs together. It was so nice to have a group of people with whom to share cooking and go out on nights on the town, etc. We created a 'kitty' for the three of us, each contributing an equal amount of money to a shared fund from which we bought food and drinks. This made things convenient since we were doing most activities together.

After a few days in Sucre, we met back up with the French guys after their pitstop in Potosi. We spent some quality time with them and Josephine, my roommate from San Pedro, who had since arrived in Sucre as well. All of us shared some truly crazy times together that generally involved booze, music, and dancing.

One night, Sofia showed us her acting video reel which included clips of very dramatic scenes of her in TV shows and movies. We laughed our asses off as she popped into a scene in a sexy black outfit, shooting people with a machine gun in an action flick. During the next scene, she was breaking up with a lover in a dramatic soap opera setting. She explained the scenes to us in English as the actors were obviously speaking German.

Even though some of us had developed a little clique, we met some new friends at the hostel. There was a dreadlocked Aussie guy that worked at the hostel that we hung out with quite a bit. The French guys were not big fans of him, referring to him as a 'Rasta' and mocking him by singing Bob Marley lyrics. When we would go out in groups, they told us not to invite him.

We met an Asian girl from Scotland, Kate, who joined us

on many of our adventures. Kate was exceptionally social, always up for a chat and a smoke. Zoe and I would see Kate again in Cusco and dine over guinea pig together weeks later on the traveling circuit. There were several other travelers whom we met and kept in touch with. The two Swedes that we had met on Night One of the salt flats tour turned up in town as well and Zoe ended up having a fling with one of them, Lars. We made fun of her because Lars, a true nonconformist, would always walk around barefoot and had filthy feet!

My Thanksgiving was spent in Sucre and it was truly memorable for both good and bad reasons—I'll start with the good. Many of us gathered for a big Thanksgiving dinner with almost everyone in the hostel participating. Sofia, Zoe, and I created a sign-up list where guests could sign up to bring a particular food item. The list included all of the traditional fixings (the non-American contingent was very excited about experiencing a Thanksgiving like they had seen in the movies) and was posted in the hostel's common area.

When the day came, everyone brought their A-game, cooking up some impressive dishes. I made my first stuffing ever—to my surprise, it actually came out great and went fast! Someone from home had emailed me a simple recipe per my request because the WiFi bandwidth wouldn't allow me to do much research. My Spanish teacher gave me a ride to the market on the back of his motorcycle to pick up the final ingredients and some funny hats for us to wear at the party.

On Thanksgiving Day, about twenty of us gathered around the table and took turns saying what we were thankful for. For many people, it was their first Thanksgiving celebration ever. It was really nice to be able to spend the holiday with people from all over the world, yet also with the traditions of home. We had to improvise, of course. Turkeys were not plentiful in Bolivia and therefore very expensive, so we went with chickens. The French guys were in charge of the chickens, and boy did they deliver! They showed up with beautifully garnished, delicious chickens encircled by roasted potatoes. Since cranberries were also impossible to find, someone made a lovely fruit sauce as a substitute. It was quite the spread!

Now for the bad news . . . unfortunately, Zoe and I were quite ill on both Thanksgiving Day and the day before. We had come down with what people referred to as the 'Bolivian flu.' Word on the street was that nobody leaves Bolivia without vomiting and diarrhea due to food poisoning, and that seemed to be true from my observations. Every member of our group of friends was a bit sick at one time or another, but Zoe and I had it pretty bad for a couple of days.

As I made my first stuffing for Thanksgiving, I battled with my queasy stomach and burned with fever. Because of how terrible I felt, I couldn't partake in any of the festive drinking that was going on which was a total buzzkill. When it was time to sit down for dinner, Zoe and I joined the group for a short time, forcing down a bit of the 'safer' food items. We then headed back to bed with serious FOMO (fear of missing out) as the crowd continued to enjoy a very festive Thanksgiving.

Zoe and I lay in bed with fever and chills for two or three days, unable to hold down much food. Fortunately, our comrades at the hostel took good care of us, bringing us medicine and simple food and checking on us all the time. It was convenient that we were staying in the same room so that people could generally steer clear of us and we could keep each other company. Not like either of us was much company—we would sleep all day and intermittently ask, "How are you feeling?" with a typical response of "Awful." This was, of course, if we weren't running to the bathroom, which was happening constantly. We were unable to hold anything down, and if we did, it went right through us.

While Zoe, Sofia, and I were originally the only people in our room, we had taken on a roommate who occupied my bottom bunk. She offered to move to allow me the bottom bunk when she realized the predicament we were in. I gratefully accepted, as simply getting out of the top bunk fast enough to make it to the bathroom was proving to be a trial in and of itself.

Sofia also moved out of our room temporarily, shacking up with one of the many men that had fallen for her. Let's just say she had her pick of the litter and she didn't always pick just one! When she would come in to visit us and bring medicine, she would tell us stories of her exploits to lift our spirits.

It seemed like every day someone else in the hostel was stricken with the Bolivian flu. I hoped it would be a one-time thing for me and I was elated once it was over! If I were a betting gal, I would bet that we acquired the food poisoning at the local market, but it could've really been anywhere. We had been spending lots of time at the market, which was a very impressive place. It was massive and chock full of vendors hawking fruits, vegetables, hot soup, and anything else you can really imagine. Like other markets I had visited on my trip thus far, this one had pyramids of fruit and vegetables that practically reached the ceiling.

Zoe and I were alone one day and had eaten aggressively from both a street vendor and from the market. We both became sick soon after, so I believe we poisoned ourselves during this outing. Specifically, I think it was the soup we ate at the local market that got us. Hygiene standards were not the same as they were back home! In fact, the hygiene standards were quite horrifying. My best hypothesis is that the water in the soup was contaminated, leading to our downfall.

Regardless, after the illness, I was a bit more careful about what I ingested!

We stayed in Sucre for a while. It was a coincidence that the different groups of friends I had made all wanted to settle down there for a bit. Our days and nights were filled with activity. Michel and Alexandre were the first to move on, and we all gathered at their hostel for a farewell dinner of llama steaks, potatoes, and vegetables. The French guys were great cooks. In fact, I was surprised at how many great cooks I had met along the way! I started to understand why people enjoyed cooking, looking at it as an activity as opposed to a chore. I was learning new methods and vowed to cook more when I eventually returned home.

Alexandre and Michel were off to the Amazon Jungle on a crazy survival mission of sorts, where they would have no food and would need to hunt and gather to survive. After the boys were gone, the girls and I continued the fun in Sucre. We went to a packed music festival one night that featured Aerosmith, Bon Jovi, and Beatles cover bands. It was absolutely hilarious and to contribute to the hilarity, I wore a jean tuxedo, which was one of my best outfits at the time. We all sang along to "It's My Life . . . It's Now or Never!!!" and "I Don't Wanna Miss a Thing." What an experience to be at a concert in a Spanish speaking country with fans from all over the world singing songs together in English! The girls and I went to a nightclub afterwards and danced until 3:00 AM.

There were several other great evenings in Sucre— goodbye celebrations, girls' nights, low key evenings chatting at the hostel, etc. When it was time for Sofia to go, we went out for happy hour to wish her well. As we laughed our asses off reminiscing around the table, we coined the terms 'Chicas Locas' (Crazy Girls) and 'South America's Best Threesome' for the three of us. We sure had some good times in Sucre and had really bonded over those last few weeks. I would miss Sofia, but would travel forward with Zoe for a bit longer. Zoe, Sofia, the French guys, and I had also discussed the potential of meeting again in Colombia around Christmas, so it wasn't necessarily goodbye for forever.

Sofia was off to the Amazon Jungle as well, where she intended to try ayahuasca. I was seriously debating trying this as well, and had not yet decided at that point. Ayahuasca is a psychedelic brew of sorts and is generally taken in a jungle setting with a shaman. Chatting with other travelers, I had learned that taking it could be a fantastic spiritual experience, something that could help you truly find yourself. On the other hand, I heard the side effects could be terrible—most notably, vomiting and diarrhea, and I had experienced enough of that recently. However, the main reason I ultimately decided against it was that I heard that some people can never go back to normal life after taking it. It changes them in a fundamental way that renders them incapable of reintegrating into society. I was really afraid that might happen to me!

My next stop would be La Paz and I planned to travel there with Zoe. Our plan was to bike down the World's Most Dangerous Road, also known as the 'Death Road.' The bike ride and the walking tour were basically the only things I needed to do in La Paz, so the visit would be short. I had heard too many stories of people getting robbed there, so I did not want to stay long. Some folks said they loved La Paz and felt completely safe there, while others said they were robbed of everything by a fake policeman who whipped out a machete. Fortunately, I had Zoe by my side, and traveling with a partner makes things safer.

Before leaving Sucre, Zoe and I took a fairly embarrassing trip to the local pharmacy. She needed cold sore medication and I needed a pregnancy test. While in Sucre, I realized that I hadn't had a menstrual cycle in quite some time, so I became a little worried. I didn't think I was pregnant but frankly speaking, there was a chance, and considering my body was not behaving the way it usually did, I needed to know for sure.

Sitting down with my iPad in the hostel lobby, Zoe and I Google translated how to say pregnancy test and cold sore medication in Spanish. Then, we made our way to the pharmacy to awkwardly request these items because, of course, we couldn't just grab them off the shelf. En route, we laughed about our predicament as we practiced our new words. Once we successfully acquired the goods, it was back to the hostel bathroom for me.

Panic set in a bit as I contemplated what a positive result would mean. At the very least, it would mean that I needed to get back to the states for proper medical care and I chose not to think any further than that at that point. The Bolivian pregnancy test was a flimsy piece of paper that was supposed to change color to indicate a positive or negative result. It cost less than a couple of bucks and needless to say, I didn't have much faith in it, but what other choice did I have?

After the recommended five minutes of waiting, I breathed a massive sigh of relief—phew! It was negative—but could I trust it? I decided I could, attributing my strange bodily functions to eating a totally new diet, sleeping on a totally different schedule, and just having an overall major change of lifestyle. Just to be sure, though, I would take another (hopefully more trustworthy) test if things continued this way.

Back to the travel plans at hand, I planned to head to Copacabana, a town on Lake Titicaca, after the pitstop in La Paz. I also intended to visit Isla del Sol, an island in the middle of Lake Titicaca. From there, I would cross the border into Peru and head to Cusco. I would spend some time there, visit Machu Picchu, and then fly to Cartagena, Colombia for

Christmas and New Year's Eve where I would reunite with Sofia and the crazy French guys!

Flying to Cartagena was a tough decision as it was expensive, but I decided it was worth it to spend the holidays with some great new friends in an amazing city. The next few border crossings had me a bit worried. Rumor had it that Peru and Colombia were sticklers when it came to proving 'onward travel.' This meant that they wanted to see proof that you would be leaving their country within a specified timeframe. Generally, this proof should be provided in the form of an airline ticket elsewhere. I did not have any onward travel booked from Colombia at that point, so I hoped that would not become an issue when crossing the border.

Per usual, I reflected as my time came to a close in Sucre. I was having such a great time with great new friends and could not believe I was almost at the three-month mark in my trip. Time was really flying which made me sad. Anxiety set in when I thought about what I would do upon my return to the states. I really needed to find something that I was passionate about and that did not involve working in a cubicle for a boring company day in and day out.

Perhaps I could get involved in the tourism/travel/hospitality industry in some way, while also applying the skills I had acquired working in finance over the years. I knew that I would also enjoy working with an organization that benefited society in some way, and I was especially interested in education. Some of the things I wanted to do would involve a big career change and a huge pay cut, and these were things that were swirling through my mind.

In the interest of enjoying the rest of my trip, I tried to forget about all of that for the time being. There would be plenty of time to worry about these things later.

23

LA PAZ, COPACABANA, ISLA DEL SOL, & PUNO

After hearing countless firsthand stories of robberies, I questioned going to La Paz at all. However, I really wanted to bike down the Death Road, so ultimately decided to take a quick trip to La Paz, check the Death Road off my list, and then get the hell out of there. My travel partner at the time, Zoe, was in the same boat, and another girl, Olga, asked if she could join us for the trip for safety purposes. Of course, we welcomed her to travel with us. Three girls are better than one if faced with a robber or kidnapper!

Taking the overnight bus from Sucre to La Paz was a very unique experience. The three of us girls that were traveling together had heard some horror stories of robberies happening on the bus, where children would run through the bus and steal things while people were sleeping, etc. So, we locked our backpacks shut (literally locked the zippers together with small padlocks), secured them to our seats (literally tied them with rope), and kept them on our laps.

Thankfully, we arrived in La Paz without incident. However, we did witness some children climbing aboard the bus at the pitstops looking around for charity (or perhaps things of value to take). You couldn't blame the poor little things—it was what they were taught to do by others which was incredibly sad.

We had also heard two different kinds of scary stories about taxi robberies. A couple we had met was robbed with a machete when taking a taxi from the bus station to their hostel in La Paz. Someone literally jumped out of the trunk and stole all of their belongings while wielding a machete. The other story involved a taxi driver taking someone to a place where the driver's partner in crime was waiting to rob you.

While we successfully avoided robbery en route to La Paz, we encountered a few other inconveniences on the bus. Of course, the bathroom wasn't working so we were forced to survive the night without peeing. There was one pitstop at a shady bathroom shack in the middle of nowhere, so we took advantage of that and then tried to go to sleep immediately without drinking any water.

The bus ride was bumpy over unpaved, windy roads, so sleep was elusive. Lack of sleep made for a bit of a cranky Day One in La Paz, as we wandered through the Witches Market suffering from fatigue and the effects of the very high altitude (shortness of breath, dizziness, etc.). We successfully accomplished our mission of the day, though, which was to book the Death Road biking trip. We arranged it for the following day so that we could minimize our time in the city, opting for a company called Vertigo based on recommendations from other travelers. This company was a step down from the most reputable one, but it was less expensive and was supposed to be just as good—budget, budget, budget!

The three of us booked into the local 'party hostel' since we were only staying two nights in La Paz. I think it is safe to say that I was the oldest person there and although it was fun, I knew I wouldn't be booking any more party hostels!

People in their twenties were partying nonstop—blasting music, doing shots, and pounding beers.

On Day Two, we were picked up at 8:00 AM for the Death Road trip. We were excited but also apprehensive. Many people had died on this road, with a few of them meeting their untimely demise just before our journey. Our guide informed us that a few weeks prior to our trip, he had attempted to rescue a fellow guide who had fallen over the edge of a ravine. The man who had fallen was still alive when our guide reached him, but he didn't end up making it. Tragedies like this were not uncommon, and a few tourists had recently fallen to their deaths into deep ravines.

Sad stories aside, this excursion was truly exceptional. We started at the top of the road (formerly known as North Yungas Road), where we were provided with bikes, full body-suits, helmets, and gloves. The drive up to this point was death-defying in and of itself. Our guide gave us a primer on what to expect—a 43-mile downhill ride on a very narrow gravel road with cliffs at every turn. The road was open to traffic and there were no guardrails.

We set off with all of this in mind. The ride was most certainly scary at times—it was easy to get distracted by the beautiful scenery and easy to lose control by picking up too much speed due to the steep slopes. While I had a few 'oh shit' moments, I clearly made it through alive! The scariest moment was when I started to skid upon braking. Safe to say my heart ended up in my stomach as I prayed that I would stop before falling over the edge of a deep gorge. We took a few breaks during the ride to drink water and heed warnings about the next bit of the road. Upon finishing the ride, the tour company took us to a hotel situated in a beautiful jungle area where we ate lunch, showered, and swam in the pool.

The day after the Death Road bike ride, I departed for Copacabana independently. Zoe, Olga, and I were all going our own separate ways to achieve different trip goals. I had booked the Bolivia Hop bus and departed at 7:00 AM. This particular bus was a bit more expensive than local busses, but it was much more convenient and safe. The reason for this is that it picks you up directly from your hostel, which takes away the worry associated with taxi robberies. The bus then drives to Copacabana, Puno and Cusco.

The beauty of this bus trip is that you don't have to do it all at once—you can stop in each place and continue on whenever you are ready. I opted to stay in Copacabana (and nearby Isla del Sol) for a few nights and then hop back on the bus to Puno and Cusco, which would take me into my next country, Peru.

Upon arrival to Copacabana, the bus crashed into a wall (it was a minor!) and dropped us off in the middle of the small lakeside town. I dropped my big backpack at a hostel that offered bag storage and went to seek out lunch. The Bolivia Hop bus deal included a boat ride to Isla del Sol, and I decided to take advantage of that and spend the first night on the island. Isla del Sol is situated in the southern part of Lake Titicaca, the world's highest navigable lake sitting at 12,000 feet of altitude. Approximately half of the lake is in Bolivia while half of it is in Peru.

Because I had not prepared for this part of my journey, I had some last-minute decisions to make. During lunch, I contemplated the situation and decided to shove some necessities into my small backpack and leave my big bag in Copacabana so I wouldn't have to lug it around the island. I wanted to get some cash, but the ATM in Copacabana was not working (big surprise!). I had 200 bolivianos to last me for two days and one night on the island, which would typically be more than enough. What I failed to realize, however, was that although it was very hot during the day, it was absolutely freezing during the night due to the altitude.

Once I got a taste of the first cold night on the island, I had to spend 100 bolivianos on an alpaca sweater and socks so that I wouldn't freeze to death. I bargained with a little old lady on the side of the road for these items and felt guilty getting her down to that price but I needed enough cash to pay for food and accommodation. Following the sweater purchase, I was left with only enough money to pay for the island hostel and eat very simply for two days before I could get back to the mainland. Ultimately, I left the island with less than the equivalent of $1.00 USD, so it all worked out perfectly but it was a close one!

As I boarded the boat en route to the island, the captain handed out beers to the passengers. He popped the caps off and threw them right into the lake. This gave me a quick shock and I realized that the people in this area had apparently not been educated about the effects of litter on the environment! To add to my state of disbelief, a child pushed the barge off the dock with a stick when it was time to depart! A quick trip over to the island ensued and as we approached, I observed the hilly landscape characterized by terraces and mazes of stairs. This unique and beautiful place is said by some to be the birthplace of the Incas.

I was dropped on the dock and started to hike up one of the many cobblestoned pathways. The island had a very primitive feel—the stone pathways were occupied by donkeys, llamas, and sheep being herded by children and women in traditional Bolivian dress.

When I arrived at the hostel, I was approached by a couple who was looking for people to share a room with them in order to get a discount. Considering my cash flow situation, I agreed to share, and we secured a large room with several beds for the three of us. It cost less than $5.00 for the night of accommodation which included breakfast. Mind you, there was no heat or shower, but what can you expect from a

Bolivian island in the middle of nowhere?! While the hostel was extremely rustic, the view of the lake was spectacular and I witnessed one of the most amazing sunrises from my room. There was a terrace with tables and chairs and a view of the lake. No matter how rustic your accommodations might be, you simply can't beat a view of the water from a hilltop terrace while sipping a beer.

My two days on the island were spent walking around and exploring. At one point, I encountered a little girl walking a llama on a leash. When I went to take a photo, she asked me for money to do so. This is the norm, and it is rude to take photos of the locals without giving them something in return. I gave her a coin, wished her a good day, and went on my way.

During my daily hikes, I stopped into little restaurants for meals, where I met some very nice folks and shared great conversation with them. There wasn't very much to do on the island and there was no internet whatsoever, so I was able to relax and catch up on some reading. I hiked quite a bit, taking in the beautiful vistas from all over the island. Admittedly, I was a bit underwhelmed by Isla del Sol in the end. Perhaps it was because I had seen so many beautiful places up to that point, so this one didn't wow me more than some others.

Upon arrival back to the mainland, I looked at a few places to stay and opted for a 'hotel' for $10.00 a night. My private room included a water view, a private bathroom, and breakfast. It was a dump by American standards but was one of the nicer places I had stayed in a while. This was my first private room of the entire trip.

What a luxury to be able to spread out and reorganize my things without six other peoples' stuff everywhere! At the same time, it was not very social like the hostels I had been staying in. However, I went out for lunch and dinner and always met other travelers during those outings. The privacy of my $10.00 hotel room gave me some downtime that I needed, as I had been moving very quickly again.

While I wasn't relaxing in my sketchy hotel room, I spent my final few days in Bolivia walking around the cute lakeside town of Copacabana. Alas, the ATM in town was still not functioning, so I exchanged some of my emergency USD to be able to fund my last few days in Bolivia.

On my final night, I embarked on what was supposed to be an easy hike to see the sunset. In classic form, I took the wrong way up and ended up scaling rockface when there was a much easier man-made path on the other side of the hill! It was very rewarding to reach the top, though, and I grabbed a beer from a local vendor to drink while I watched the sun go down. There were several Bolivians hanging out and getting drunk at the top of this hill—one pair in particular was drinking hard liquor and beer while chain-smoking cigarettes.

The children of the families that were hanging around were throwing glass bottles off the top of the mountain and smashing them and this seemed to be completely acceptable. There was so much litter everywhere, and it made me sad that such a beautiful place wasn't being more well preserved.

The following morning, I hopped on the bus to Cusco, Peru with a pitstop in Puno. There was a group of six travelers on this bus and we all visited the man-made floating islands of Puno—87 islands made out of reeds where people actually live. It was very cool, but it was also a total tourist trap filled with gift shops and women pushing their wares on you.

The group of us from the bus had dinner together in Puno and played a card game to compete for the back seat of the bus. As the winner of this card game, I was able to lay across the back seat while the other six had to sit in normal seats for the overnight journey to Cusco. We all agreed to keep the bathroom window open as it was very stinky, but this made for a freezing trip. I bundled myself up in the grungy blankets provided by the bus company, which I'm sure were used by countless other people without being washed. But you gotta do what you gotta do!

I tried to focus on Cusco and my plan to visit Machu Picchu. I thought of how I would most likely do the 5-day Salkantay trek, which is intense, but sounded amazing. My thoughts also went to Christmas Eve, when I would fly to Cartagena, Colombia and reunite with some of my traveler friends and a friend from home. I was looking forward to all of these things!

24

CUSCO / MACHU PICCHU

The bus arrived in Cusco at 5:00 AM but we were allowed to sleep on the bus until 6:00 AM (ahh, such luxury, especially since I had prime real estate!). I dragged myself to a hostel at 6:00 AM and paid the half-night rate so that I could go to sleep for a few more hours.

During the first few days in Cusco, I wandered around the city and reunited with some other travelers that I had met along my journey. As chance would have it, I was able to meet up with my friends Josephine (from Switzerland, whom I met in San Pedro) and Anne (from the Netherlands, whom I met in Buenos Aires), to get some socializing in.

One day, Josephine and I visited the Pisco 'Museum,' which is really just a Pisco bar where you can make your own Pisco Sour. Of course, we partook and then proceeded to have a fun, crazy night out in one of the local establishments on the square! It was on this night that I met Guillaume, an outrageously handsome French man. As Josephine and I were chatting, I met his gaze across the bar and was struck by his good looks. He looked like he had just walked out of a magazine ad for men's cologne.

Guillaume and I continued to lock eyes until he finally came over to say hello. He invited us to play darts with him and his friends. Guillaume communicated in Spanish, and after some small talk I learned that he could speak only Spanish and French. However, he had some friends that could speak Spanish and English and considering Josephine spoke French, Spanish, English, and Swiss German, there were translators available when needed.

We all drank and laughed and played darts while getting to know each other in Spanglish. It was great fun and we decided to proceed across the square to the local nightclub. More laughter and dancing ensued and I'll leave the rest up to your imagination!

My daytime wanderings took me up cobblestone hills lined with whitewashed buildings adorned with blue trim. Cusco is such a quaint colonial city abound with these white stucco buildings, terra cotta rooftops, and imposing cathedrals. While I wasn't wandering the streets, I was planning my next move.

After some deliberation regarding the Machu Picchu trek, I booked the 4-day Inca Jungle Trek as opposed to the 5-day Salkantay trek. I made this decision for a few reasons: 1. I had a head cold at the time and the Salkantay was supposed to be freezing and snowy, 2. The Salkantay is much more hardcore and I was not feeling in the best of shape, 3. I was confident that I could survive for four days in the jungle better than I could for five days at high, freezing altitudes, especially considering I planned to leave my large pack behind and bring only my small backpack.

Once my decision was made, I booked the excursion through the activities desk at my hostel. It was a very simple process and I got ready to depart the following day.

On Day One of the trek, I was picked up by a van at my hostel, and we headed to the first activity, a mountain bike ride similar to the one down the Death Road in Bolivia. The van ride to the start of the bike ride was terrifying, involving several near head-on collisions around hairpin turns. Of course, the roads were narrow and bordered by steep cliffs with no guardrails.

During the van ride, I met my comrades for this 4-day excursion, which included a group of six South African guys and an English couple. The group was great and we all got along very well. We were also all in the same boat in terms of fitness and tolerance level, so we ended up enjoying the trek and also suffering together at certain points.

While the bike ride that we started with would most certainly be considered dangerous, the road was paved and it was a bit safer than the one in Bolivia. After the bike ride, the agenda had us going on a whitewater rafting trip—my first ever. Because of this, I was a bit nervous, but it was fine as the rapids were not too ferocious that day. Our guide even said we could jump into the river at one point as we paddled through a calm area, so we all jumped in with all of our clothes on. It was a fun and successful first day.

We spent the remainder of our days walking along narrow mountain roads and trails, sometimes with trucks barreling by less than a foot away. The altitude was tremendous, so we would munch on coca leaves to alleviate the effects. The group would stop for lunch at places in the middle of nowhere. Sometimes little old ladies would be selling their wares—things like bracelets or beautifully colored linens. At one point on the trail, we encountered a traditionally dressed old woman selling bottled water that appeared to be open already. No thanks!

Our nightly accommodations were rustic hostels. On Night One, there was an option for a cold shower, which I took advantage of considering how sweaty I was. It was not too bad since we were in the jungle and it was very warm out. We were served dinner and we socialized over a few beers before calling it a night early due to exhaustion.

We encountered such fascinating things along this physically challenging, yet rewarding 4-day trek through the jungle. One day, we had to cross a raging river by sitting in a very sketchy chair hanging from a cable that ran from one side of the river to the other. It was like a ski lift type of apparatus and let's just say you were a goner if it failed.

We continued to hike along narrow trails with no hand rails and plunging gorges inches away—one wrong step and you're dead. Occasionally, we would get to rest at pitstops and sometimes these pitstops would even have hammocks. I had really mixed feelings about resting in these hammocks. On one hand, I was grossed out by how many sweaty people had likely laid their heads in them, but on the other hand, I was exhausted so did not care!

Day Two of the excursion involved a long day of trekking in the rain, but it was incredible, as we hiked part of the Inca Trail among the beautiful mountains. Our guide paused along the way to give us history lessons and to show us the abundant coca leaves growing on the side of the trail. At the end of Day Two, we visited hot springs where we swam around and rinsed off all of that day's sweat. The hot water felt so good on my sore muscles.

Our guide gave us the option to continue trekking for one hour after the hot springs break or take a bus ride for about $3.00 each to reach the next town. We all opted to take the $3.00 bus ride, which is hilarious, and again had me appreciating the fact we were all in similar physical condition. The crew and I went to a 'nightclub' in the town that night where we were the only patrons. The DJ played loud music and we drank cocktails while hitting the empty dance floor that was decorated with a disco ball and lit by strobe lights.

Day Three began with optional ziplining and I opted out

of this activity as it cost $30.00 and I had already ziplined in my life. While I had enjoyed ziplining before, I didn't feel the need to have the same experience again for $30.00 when I could put that money toward extending my trip. While the others ziplined, I chilled out at a lovely farm and read my book under the shade of a jungle tree.

When the ziplining activities were complete, we trekked for a few hours to the town of Aguas Calientes, near Machu Picchu. At times, we were walking along a train route and a train would blast by just feet away. In Aguas Calientes, we had dinner and prepared for a 4:00 AM wakeup for the final push to Machu Picchu. Most of us took the bus to Machu Picchu, as we were dead tired from the previous few days and I personally wanted to ensure that I could make the final trek to Wayna Picchu, where there promised to be legendary views.

The day finally came for our trek's climax at Machu Picchu. What a tremendous sight to see! The clouds lifted just in time for us to take in the beautiful views upon our arrival. I was in awe of how the Incas were able to build this city in such a remote, mountainous area with very basic tools. Every stone was perfectly set in its place.

The crew and I spent the day wandering around the ruins and then I embarked on a solo mission to hike up Wayna Picchu. Wayna Picchu is the large mountain that rises over Machu Picchu (infamously pictured in the background of most photos of the ruins) and from which you can take in unrivaled views of Machu Picchu. Hiking Wayna Picchu required obtaining a ticket in advance and I was so glad I had the foresight to do so as only a certain number of visitors are allowed to make the steep ascent each day.

While it was totally worth it, I had to keep reminding myself on the way up, "You can do this, keep going, this is the final uphill battle." My body was sore but my spirits were high. It was truly rewarding to reach the top and take in what is rightly proclaimed as a wonder of the world.

Back in Aguas Calientes, we all killed some time together drinking coffees (and then graduating to Pisco Sours) while we waited for our train back to Cusco. We reminisced on the great experience we had together during those four days in the jungle. All of us were covered in mosquito bites, with some of the boys in particularly rough shape due to wearing shorts on the first day. I couldn't even look at their swollen, oozing ankles without feeling sick! When the train arrived, we went our separate ways, each of our journeys continuing in different directions.

While I awaited my Christmas Eve flight to Cartagena, Colombia, I spent a few more days in Cusco. There, I treated myself a bit more than usual, visiting the good restaurants in town each day. I had been so tight with my budget to that point so I figured I could splurge a little and enjoy!

For my last meal in Cusco, I met up with Zoe and Kate who had just arrived in town. We dined at one of the finer restaurants, known to serve guinea pig. Guinea pig was common fare and you could eat it anywhere but I decided to do it at a classy establishment to reduce the chances of getting sick. Zoe screamed and Kate looked on in silent horror when they brought it to the table in full animal form. I laughed and took a bite while the girls grimaced—it tasted like chicken!

As my time in Peru came to a close, I looked forward to Colombia where I would reunite with some friends and spend the holidays. My friend Mia, from home, would be meeting me in Cartagena. She planned to arrive a few days early and do some exploring of her own before meeting up with me and my newfound pals for Christmas and New Year's.

Mia was an avid, adventurous traveler so I had no qualms about her figuring out the situation and meeting me at a particular hostel at a defined time. Sofia would also be meeting me at this hostel on Christmas Eve, so I described the girls to one another in case they crossed paths before my arrival.

25

CARTAGENA, COLOMBIA

I don't even know where to begin when it comes to Cartagena . . . what a crazy place!

After taking three flights, I arrived in Cartagena on Christmas Eve, somehow managing to get into Colombia without proof of onward travel. Making my way to the hostel, I was excited to reunite with Mia and Sofia.

To my delight, they had already met and were hanging out in the common area when I arrived. I had not seen Mia in about four months, and I was a dirty, scraggly backpacker by this point. When I walked in wearing my homemade shorts that I had cut from a pair of jeans, I could tell she was proud.

The three of us girls grabbed some dinner and drinks and then continued on to have quite the Christmas Eve celebration. We attended a big party hosted by a hostel that was going to be our new home in a few days. All accommodations in the city were booked solid for the holidays . . . fortunately Sofia had arrived a few days early and pounded the pavement to find this place. It was your classic backpacker factory/party hostel, which I had sworn off of after La Paz, but we had no choice.

Nevertheless, word on the street was that the Christmas Eve party at this hostel was supposed to be the best in town, so we made our way there after a few attempts to patronize some local joints that were closed. The party turned out to be insane and we danced the night away (quite literally) on the rooftop with hundreds of other people. Sweaty bodies swayed amidst clouds of smoke and bright lights. It was a heathen-like atmosphere where sex, drugs, and rock and roll were the norm. I'll leave the rest of this scene to your imagination . . .

Christmas Day was spent primarily in recovery mode, but Mia and I managed to take a nice walk through the vibrant streets and along the old walls of the city. Antique lanterns and wrought iron balconies overflowing with beautiful flowers adorned the colorful facades. As had become our daily habit, we hit up one of the many mango stands around town for some freshly cut mango.

Cartagena was very well decorated for the holiday season and there was a huge Christmas tree on display in one of the squares. We took some Christmas photos in front of the tree for posterity as the photos from the Christmas Eve party would likely never surface again! Mia and I enjoyed a Christmas dinner of chicken, rice, crackers, and local beer at a food festival that we stumbled upon. In our hungover state, we couldn't be bothered to seek out anything else. The ambiance was lovely, at least, as the food festival was set in a park bejeweled with beautiful Christmas lights.

It certainly didn't feel like Christmas in the 100-degree heat and, indeed, we kept forgetting it was Christmas, but there were plenty of drunken Australians at the hostel screaming out "Merry Christmas" all day to remind us. We each called home to touch base with our families (albeit briefly due to terrible WiFi) and everyone was happy to hear that we were alive and well.

According to plan, the three of us moved to the party

hostel and stayed there for a few days. It was both comical and hellish at the same time. In fact, we fondly referred to the place as 'the hellhole.' Mia, Sofia, and I resided in a dorm room with four beds total. The fourth bed was occupied by a male roommate who worked at the hostel.

Our room had a secondary 'door' (and by door, I mean open entryway with some beads hanging from the threshold) that led to a hallway where there were shared bathroom facilities and showers. Crudely painted on the wall of our room was the phrase, "Don't use more than 1 bed . . . if you do it, you pay for it," in addition to a no smoking marijuana symbol. There was no air conditioning (did I mention how hot it was?!) and the place was filthy. Sofia even stepped in a pile of vomit one night.

On the bright side, this place made for a good party spot and we were guaranteed admission into the rooftop parties for free! Believe it or not, this was quite the perk, as people were literally trying to break the doors down on New Year's Eve to get in.

There was a pack of Argentinian guys staying in the room next door and they did not sleep for days. They would scream and yell all night and walk right into our room whenever they felt like it. One night, a guy walked into our room and asked "Quieres sexo?" ("Do you want to have sex?"). Sofia screamed, "Get the hell out of here!!!" in her very stern German accent which scared him away as Mia and I laughed hysterically. As if the hostel's constant blasting electronic music wasn't enough for these guys, they rented a commercial-sized speaker to put in their room and cranked it until 7:00 AM each morning. If you are wondering how they kept going, just keep in mind we were in Colombia!

While in Cartagena, we reunited with Alexandre and Michel, the crazy French guys. They were skinny and unkempt from their time in the Amazon and had some hilarious stories to tell. They told tales of sneaking candy along and stealing food from one another on the brink of starvation. I was so glad Mia had the opportunity to meet them. One of the first questions they asked her was if she would rather have sex with a llama or eat flamingo for the rest of her life. She quickly chose the llama option and they approved.

The five us discovered what we referred to thereafter as our 'favorite plaza,' where we went for cheap street food and cocktails to start each evening. For around ten bucks each, we feasted on delicious grilled meats and drank several huge mojitos while hanging in a charming outdoor plaza with twinkling lights in the trees.

One night after leaving the plaza, we experienced your classic shakedown by the police as we headed to a nightclub in town. About ten of us were walking late at night and two motorcycles carrying three policemen stopped and searched everyone. It was a bit unsettling at the time because someone may or may not have been in possession of something, but fortunately, they let us go on our way. I'll never forget the image of the boys with their hands up against the wall getting frisked!

During Mia's final days in Colombia, we took in more of the city's sights and spent a day out on the water. In addition to grandiose cathedrals and picturesque town squares, there were some other, more unconventional sights that we witnessed. Take the 'modern day phone booth' as Mia coined it, a sight commonly seen around Cartagena—this is a cell phone stand with several used cell phones available from which you can make a call for a certain price. These stands were commonly operated by women nursing their children out in the open (just for the record, I don't think there is anything wrong this and am simply pointing out the phenomenon).

Another frequently sighted spectacle was the 'walking store,' a man selling coffee, cigarettes, candy, and drugs disguised as lollipops from a tray dangling around his neck. Word on the street was that the high-quality drugs were saved for export, though, and not sold at these 'walking stores.'

During our day out on the water, the girls went diving while I went snorkeling. I was not certified to dive at the time but was considering getting certified at one of my next stops. Mia had shared the name of the outfit she dove with before she arrived in Cartagena. She highly recommended it and I planned to look them up if and when I visited that town, which was very likely.

When the day of Mia's departure came, she and I visited with the French guys on the rooftop of their hostel so she could say her goodbyes. I was thrilled that she had hit it off and created a bond with them. Photos from that day show us looking very tan and blonde, with nightclub bracelets still garnishing our wrists.

With Mia gone, four of us remained, and we soaked up those last few days in Cartagena. One day, Sofia, Alexandre, and I took an adventurous trip to Playa Blanca (a popular beach) using local transport. The journey to the beach involved your standard death ride in busses and 'taxis' (old jalopies that seem like they are from the year 1950) driving at outrageous speeds, constantly honking and slamming on the brakes.

Looking out the windows, it was not uncommon to see men riding donkeys with milk crates hanging off the sides to hold their cargo, and children riding bikes either way too big or too small for them. Colorful laundry hanging to dry and litter strewn about the streets were becoming familiar backdrops.

We found ourselves a spot on the beach and relaxed in the sand for the day, napping, reading, and swimming. It was lovely to get a taste of the aqua Caribbean water. The place was absolutely packed with tourists, which may have been driven by the fact that it was a holiday week. In the afternoon, a long line formed for the boat back to Cartagena . . . this was a total shitshow, so we opted to take the taxi and bus route back.

Before I knew it, New Year's Eve had rolled around. Sofia and I dressed up in our best outfits and donned glittery headbands for the occasion. I couldn't believe the year 2015 was about to be upon us. Sofia, Alexandre, Michel, and I went for dinner to start the evening's festivities. Two of the four of us (the boys) did not make it to the fireworks display that night due to overconsumption of Aguardiente before, during, and after dinner!

Sofia and I watched the fireworks and rang in the new year from atop the old city walls of Cartagena. It was a surreal experience. We returned to the good old rooftop for their crazy NYE party, where people were literally stampeding to get in and men were holding the doors shut against the crowds.

Now that 2015 had arrived, it was time to make a move. I would miss Cartagena, which had proven to be such a colorful city both literally and figuratively. I would never forget the party time atmosphere everywhere, with the streets perpetually filled with music and people. My next stop would be a surf camp located about five hours northeast of Cartagena. Sofia and I planned to travel there together.

From the surf camp, I was not sure yet. I had booked a four-day boating excursion to Panama via the San Blas

Islands that would depart on January 20th. My only commitment was to arrive to the port on January 18th, so I would visit some other places in the meantime. I was super, super excited about this part of my journey as I love boating and anything to do with the ocean!

26

COSTEÑO BEACH, MINCA, AND TAGANGA

The next few days were spent in various places on the Caribbean coast of Colombia and characterized by what I can only call 'seriously local' transport. Sofia and I left Cartagena on a local bus to Santa Marta, fortunate enough to get this bus at the last minute after all of the shuttles were sold out.

Upon getting off the bus, we met two Canadian guys as we were walking around aimlessly trying to figure out how to get to our final destination of Taganga. These guys were headed to the same place, so we shared a taxi with them.

Sofia and I spent one night in Taganga, a little coastal town near Tayrona National Park, as the surf camp we were headed to didn't have availability until the following night. Our night in Taganga was spent hanging out on the seawall with our new Canadian friends, drinking Aguardiente after a dinner of ceviche. While the town was your standard slightly seedy beach town, the sunset was glorious and we all appreciated the natural beauty the ocean had to offer.

The following day, Sofia and I made our way to Costeño Beach Surf Camp via several modes of transport—two local busses followed by motorcycle taxis. The second crazy local bus, characteristically decorated with colorful tasseled curtains and fuzz-lined fittings dropped us off on the side of the road at an intersection. From there, we hopped on motorcycle (moto) taxis that would take us to the camp due to its remote location.

A moto taxi is exactly what you would imagine—a motorcycle available for you to ride on the back of to your destination. Riding on the back of a moto taxi with a massive backpack on while the driver holds your small backpack is muy peligroso (very dangerous), but quite the sight to see! Arriving unscathed, we arranged to sleep in hammocks for the first few nights and would then move into a bunk room for the following two nights based on availability. We secured two hammocks next to one another, each equipped with a mosquito net, dropped our bags, and went to check the place out.

Costeño Beach was a beautiful oasis on the Caribbean—untouched coastline with white sand and turquoise water—not a bad place to spend a few days. Because it is so remote, all guests eat all of their meals there. A bell is rung when each meal is ready and everybody rushes to line up. Sofia and I found this a bit unusual and did not rush to get in line for our first meal there. However, we soon learned that the place was over capacity so if you didn't get a good spot in line, your plate of food would likely be missing some ingredients!

The staff was permanently stoned and could not be bothered to answer questions or God forbid, make you a smoothie to have with your rum (which you were paying for, of course!). A bag of weed was easier to acquire than a bottle of water. There was a charging station which looked like a total fire hazard—power strips plugged into other power strips with ten cell phone cords hanging off of each. Accommodation-wise, we roughed it for a few days at the camp, but it didn't feel like roughing it due to the beautiful surroundings, which totally made up for the service.

We had plenty of quality girl time and a lot of laughs, but something felt a bit off with both of us. Even though we were in paradise, we felt a little depressed, or more specifically, tired and unmotivated. After discussing this amongst ourselves and with some others, we realized that these feelings were probably side effects of the malaria pills we had been taking. Considering the pros and cons, we both decided to stop taking them, and I soon felt better mentally.

Unfortunately, the sea was too rough during the entire four days we spent at Costeño Beach for us to surf or take surf lessons. I attempted a swim at one point, but got knocked down repeatedly by the strong surf! Because there was no WiFi (and not much electricity or running water for that matter), we spent our time hanging out in hammocks, reading, and just chilling on the beach. It was very relaxing to be totally unplugged.

One day, we took a day trip to Tayrona National Park, a coastal park with beautiful jungle trails and beaches. After moto taxi rides to the entrance of the park, we hiked for an hour and a half to reach the beach. It was high season so it was crazy getting into the park due to the fact that there is a daily capacity limit and there were lots of tourists converging on the place. We made it in before it hit capacity, though, and ultimately found a nice, secluded spot on the beach to hang out for the day. Massive boulders, smooth and rounded from the strong sea, rested along the coastline.

When it was time to head back, Sofia and I triple rode on a moto taxi, which was a first!

Sofia and I said our final goodbyes at the surf camp which was, of course, bittersweet. We had spent so much quality time together but it was time to move on to our next independent adventures. I headed to a little mountain town in

Colombia called Minca, and she headed to Costa Rica. She planned to spend some time with my friend Mia's family at their vacation home in Costa Rica, which she and Mia had arranged during our time together in Cartagena.

I hopped on a moto taxi, which by that point I had become accustomed to, and set off for Minca. This time, the driver carried my large backpack, and I carried my small one, which made me feel safer. The moto taxi dropped me off in the city of Santa Marta and I took a colectivo from there to Minca.

A colectivo is technically defined as a small public bus, but can take many shapes and sizes based on my experience. This particular one was similar to a paddy wagon . . . eight of us rode in the barred bed of a pickup truck through the bumpy windy mountainous roads to Minca. This ride was an adventure in and of itself as many of my rides were!

Minca was breathtaking—a tiny little town with one main dirt, pothole-filled road. I stayed in a hostel that was located atop a massive hill. The only way to reach it was to hike up the hill which was quite difficult with the huge backpack, but worth it. The sunsets from up there were some of the best I have ever seen, with vivid colors splashed over dark mountain landscapes.

Because the hostel's location was so remote, most travelers ate the majority of their meals there, similar to Costeño Beach. The food was muy rico (delicious) and you didn't have to stand in line to get it! I had a 'private cabana' which was basically a rustic yurt for two nights and a dorm bed for one night. The private cabana was $15.00 per night. Can't beat it!

During my time in Minca, I hiked through a bamboo forest to a waterfall one day. Another day, I visited a coffee plantation with an English girl I met while watching the sunset the night before. We had gotten to chatting at sunset, gone for a cocktail at a random shack on the side of the hill, and arranged a day trip to the coffee farm for the following day. We took moto taxis there and walked the hour and a half back. During our day trip, we toured the farm, learned about the production process, and sipped on some delicious coffee.

After a few days in Minca, it was back to Taganga for me, where I would complete an open water diving course with the company that my friend Mia recommended. I was a little nervous about diving but knew it was a fear that I had to conquer! All of the divers I knew absolutely loved the sport so I was excited to see what the fuss was all about. The course I chose involved heading to a remote beach in Tayrona National Park by boat where I would sleep in a hammock for two nights and learn to dive for three days.

I was so excited about the dive course that I almost forgot about my upcoming boat trip to Panama. That was until I received a very amusing email which included an itinerary from the company I would be boating with. The part of the itinerary regarding the border crossing said in big, bold, red lettering, '**At this point the army may check all the luggage —be 100% sure you don't have any drugs, they will find it and you will go to jail 10 years**.'

As I chuckled, I stopped myself, wondering if there was any chance I had a forgotten joint stashed somewhere in one of my bags.

27

LEARNING TO DIVE IN SPANISH

The dive certification course I chose was marketed as a three-day safari in Tayrona National Park. I wanted to start on a Sunday, but they preferred that I start on Monday. Because of this, I was able to negotiate staying at the dive center for free for one night and waiving the 5% credit card fee for my 'inconvenience.' The accommodation at the dive center was basic to say the least, but it was free, so I was not complaining!

In hindsight, the room I stayed in basically looked like a murder den. It was furnished with two sets of dilapidated bunkbeds with old, yellowed, sunken-in mattresses. I distracted myself in this murder den by watching the required video for the course on the laptop they loaned me.

The following morning, the lead instructor and I walked down the dirt road to the coast, where we boarded a boat headed for a remote beach. I met the other two people that would be taking the course with me—an awesome Colombian couple a bit older than me who were on holiday. At first, the instructor spoke to the couple in Spanish and to me in broken English. However, once he realized I could understand the couple and was speaking to them in Spanish, he asked me if it was okay for him to drop the English part of his instruction. I told him that would be fine as long as he could speak slowly and didn't mind plenty of clarifying questions. I was nervous, but proud that I was learning to dive in Spanish!

We arrived to the very isolated, beautiful beach which was a classic crescent shaped, white sand beach surrounded by dazzling turquoise waters. An open structure with a thatched roof housed several hammocks, and a separate shack housed the kitchen. There was one more small shack with a basic bathroom and no showers.

Langostas (huge grasshoppers) were perched on every surface. Lizards and bees were also plentiful and a boa constrictor had been roaming around the day before our arrival. It was quite the adventure, and I had to overcome some fears of wildlife to be able to sleep there in my hammock!

Once we dropped our bags and picked out our hammocks, we met the other three instructors and the cook, who were the only other inhabitants of this remote beach. One instructor was a pretty blonde American girl, one was her Colombian boyfriend, and the other was a blonde, dreadlocked Australian guy. All of our meals and snacks would be had there and provided as part of the course. The cook, an elderly Colombian man named Toto, took a liking to me and gave me extra coffee and cookies each day, which was fantastic and made the already sunny days shine brighter.

The first day of the course involved learning about the diving equipment and doing some exercises underwater. The exercises included taking the regulator out of your mouth and taking your mask off while twenty-five feet underwater.

Fortunately, I had worked myself up so much about this that when it actually happened, it wasn't so bad.

During the second day of the course, we performed some different exercises—breathing your buddy's air, practicing emergency ascents, taking all equipment off and putting it back on while in the water, etc. We also completed three dives around some beautiful coral reef and I saw some brilliantly colored fish and coral. It was an eye-opening experience to be in this whole new world under the sea. Observing the life in this immense part of our world that we never really see or think about was truly incredible.

Over the course's three days, we completed six dives in total. There was only one point at which I became borderline panicked. While out for a dive with two instructors in rough, unclear waters, I got lost, ending up on my own. The instructors were disorganized that day and the buddy system did not work as planned. Being lost underwater, in murky waters at that, is not exactly a comforting experience! I remained calm for the most part, slowly ascending while looking around for someone else. Ultimately, I located the crew without completely hyperventilating.

During the evenings, we would sit by the campfire and chat over a beer or two. The Colombian couple helped me with my Spanish and I helped them with some English. The three of us were all proud to be officially NAUI certified once the three day 'safari' concluded. As we parted ways on the dirt road in front of the dive shop back in Taganga, we promised to meet up for a drink in Cartagena when I passed through there again.

After the dive course, I spent one more night in Taganga before heading back to Cartagena. I chose a hostel with views of the ocean and mountains and soaked up my last night in town. There was a book swap at the hostel, which was fairly typical, and I swapped my Colombia book for a Panama one since my next stop was fast approaching. Then, I treated myself to a delicious dinner—a whole fish beautifully seasoned and served with rice.

I could not believe how fast time was flying and as usual, I reflected on my time away thus far and my next steps. Most importantly, I had to prepare for the four-day boat trip to Panama. I would buy the necessities for the journey in Cartagena, as that was where the trip would commence. A shuttle was scheduled to pick me up in Cartagena in a couple of days for the long drive to the port of Turbo, Colombia.

I was eager to start the boat trip through the San Blas Islands. While this trip was on the forefront of my mind, I also thought ahead to the time I would spend in Panama. There, I planned to see the Panama Canal, get a few more dives in, and explore the country for a while. My loose itinerary had me heading to Costa Rica after that. The craziest part of my plan at this point was that I had to start thinking about heading home! I figured that I would most likely fly home from San Jose, Costa Rica in early March, but this was still very much up in the air.

While I was excited about the next part of my trip, I was also feeling very anxious about something else entirely. A very close friend of mine, Grace, had recently Facetimed me to ask me personally to be in her upcoming wedding. Of course, I was honored, and initially said yes. I most certainly wanted to be a part of the wedding, but I was very stressed about the cost. As any woman who has been in a wedding party knows, the cost of bachelorette parties, wedding showers, dresses, favors, food, décor, etc. adds up very quickly.

So, after thinking it over, I had to back out. I felt awful telling her that I could not be in the wedding, but she was very understanding. The fact was, all of the pre-wedding festivities would be taking place soon after my arrival home and I had no idea how long it would take me to get a new job and generate an income. This was definitely one of the biggest sacrifices I had to make as a result of my travels, but I was so grateful that my friend was understanding.

28

COLOMBIA & SAN BLAS ISLANDS

T he trip from Colombia to Panama via the San Blas Islands was a spectacular adventure! The islands were literally some of the most beautiful I had ever seen, rivaling some very exotic favorites in Thailand. This trip was not for the faint of heart, though! The company made it clear that this was a 'backpacking trip' and not a cruise, but I don't think anything could have prepared the participants for the boat rides that followed.

On Day One, a shuttle picked me up from my hostel in Cartagena according to plan. The day's itinerary called for an 11-hour van ride from Cartagena to Turbo. The good news was that there were some fun people in the van, particularly two hilarious (and handsome) Aussie guys who were guaranteed to make the trip a good time. Being stuck in a very cramped van whilst smooshed up against the hottest Aussie you've seen in a long time is really not so bad.

There was a pitstop for lunch along the way and several of us grabbed beers for the rest of the laughter-filled ride. The driver had to pull over during the journey so that we could all pee on the side of the road. It was clear upon arrival to Turbo that it was a very sketchy town. The hostel for that night (included as part of the trip) was horrible, complete with filthy beds and creepy mulleted men hanging around the stoop.

Each person had to pick a roommate for the night, as each room had two twin beds, and I ended up rooming with a Canadian guy around my age. The room situation was slightly awkward as the shower and toilet were not separated from the rest of the room. We worked this out by taking turns while the other person went out to spend time in the common area.

During this one and only night in Turbo, the whole group banded together for safety and ventured out for dinner. It was an early night as we had a big day ahead.

On Day Two, we prepared for departure to the islands. As we waited by a very smelly fishing dock to board the first boats, we 'waterproofed' our belongings by putting everything into huge double-bagged Hefty trash bags. Our group of about twenty-five people was divided into two subgroups and we climbed into our two vessels, which I can only describe as glorified dinghies. Each boat had about five wooden benches for seating and we crowded in.

We embarked on the 3.5-hour boat ride from Turbo to a place called Capurgana in extremely rough seas which had almost caused our trip to be canceled. People screamed as the boats lurched over eight-foot swells and slammed down with such force that we were all bruised and battered by the end of the first leg. It was a constant Bang!, Bang!, Bang! as we crashed through the waves, getting serious air and taking on plenty of seawater.

The girl next to me started crying and I reassured her that we would be okay even though I wasn't so sure about that. The journey definitely seemed unsafe and I contemplated the likelihood of reaching land if we were to capsize. Terrified screams turned into pained groans toward the end of the trip. Regrettably, it was too wet to take out a camera to capture any of this, but it will forever live on in my memory.

During the first day, we made a pitstop in the little beach town of Capurgana to use the bathroom, and another pitstop for a military checkpoint, ultimately arriving to a town called Sapzurro where we would spend the night. Men armed with machine guns checked our identification at the military checkpoint and sent us on our way.

During the pee stop, the crew asked for volunteers to move from the front to the back of the boat. Considering the front takes the hardest beating when the boat slams down over the waves, I thought moving to the back would be a good idea and volunteered. I quickly learned that the back had a different issue—the waves simply pummel you the entire time to the point that you can't even open your eyes and you feel like you are swimming in the ocean rather than riding in a boat. Mind you, while you are being pummeled by waves, you are straddling a massive backpack wrapped up in a Hefty trash bag.

It was insane and all you could do was laugh and hope the waters would calm down for the next part of the trip. A guy sitting next to me in the back wore a diving mask so that he could keep his eyes open—pure comedy!

Upon arrival in Sapzurro, we were all delighted to get off the boats for the day. Some folks helped to unload baggage while some started to walk around and explore. The aforementioned hot Aussie guy was helping to unload bags when he jammed his hand in between the dock and the boat as the boat rocked violently due to the rough seas. I heard him yell out a profanity and looked over to see the top of his pinky literally hanging off. It was a disgusting sight.

Considering we were in the middle of nowhere, with no serious medical facilities around, he was rushed back to

Capurgana with his hand on ice with hopes that there would be sufficient medical attention there. He sat in the boat awaiting departure as his buddy gathered their belongings. Not only did he have to endure that very rough boat ride again, he had to pay $600.00 since he and his friend were the only passengers. We later learned that they had to send him back to Turbo for surgery. Needless to say, he and his friend did not end up making it on the rest of the trip which was a total buzzkill.

Sapzurro was not too exciting and mainly served as a resting point before we got to the glorious San Blas Islands. I bunked up with three other girls and we had some dinner, drinks, and girl talk together. They were just as disappointed as I was that the Aussie guys were gone, so we commiserated during our little slumber party! After the full day of punishing boat rides, we were absolutely beat and hit the sack early, hoping the sea wouldn't be as angry the following day.

On Day Three of the excursion, we departed from Sapzurro and finally arrived at the glorious San Blas Islands. En route, we experienced a very interesting border crossing into Panama—we all had to jump out of the boats into waist deep water with our trash-bagged belongings, bring them to shore, and lay everything out for dogs to check. Then we had to manage to get back on board the boats without the aid of a dock. It was completely bizarre and I was really starting to understand why the company emphasized the fact this was not a cruise.

We spent our first day in San Blas snorkeling and relaxing on a completely deserted island, and then visiting a village of the indigenous people, the Kuna. In the Kuna village, traditionally dressed women peeked out over the fences of their thatched roofed homes and naked children played in the dirt roads. We kicked soccer balls with the kids to their amusement. Someone in our group coined the term 'The I Don't Know What I Want to be When I Grow up Club' which was very fitting for us all.

The following few days were spent on several different remote, stunning islands. Our accommodations were hammocks under thatch-roofed huts. The bathroom facilities contained toilets that were basically slabs of wood with holes that went straight down into the ocean. Dinner was comprised of freshly caught shellfish each night.

Of course, there were more bone-rattling boat rides from island to island but they were so worth it. Daily activities included snorkeling, reading, playing volleyball, etc., etc. You could have a local Kuna man climb a tree and retrieve a coconut for you for $1.00. I drank several virgin coconut waters by day and several rum and coconuts by night. While still in civilization, someone had given us the tip to buy a bottle of rum to pour into your coconuts.

In the evenings, we would feast on locally caught squid and crab and then sit around the bonfire sharing stories. One day, we organized what we called the 'Beer Olympics,' which included games like coconut bowling, coconut throwing, plank walking, flip cup, and peg leg races. A great deal of time was spent simply lounging on the beach and taking it all in. We would often see luxury yachts offshore which would ignite slight pangs of jealousy that were offset by pride in our mode of travel.

On Day Five, as we were cruising along to our next island at a very high speed, we had a terrifying experience, somehow managing to crash into another boat on the open water. All of the passengers on my boat saw it coming, but thought maybe the captains of the boats were playing a practical joke. As we sped head on toward the other boat, both captains tried to correct and avoid each other at the last minute. They coincidentally kept correcting the wrong way without decreasing speed and then BOOM!!! Thank God, at the last second, the captains corrected enough to soften the blow and avoid a complete disaster, but there was still a solid impact.

When I realized what was happening, I considered jumping out of the boat but it was too late, so I just put my head between my knees, closed my eyes, and braced for it. Everyone was okay, but the boats sustained some damage. The captains had to retrieve a significant amount of debris out of the water before we were able to continue along. We celebrated once we arrived at the next island in one piece, but we were certainly shaken.

Finally, the trip ended in Carti, a coastal town on the mainland of Panama. We disembarked and crammed into 4x4's for the 3-hour drive to Panama City where we would be dropped off at a recommended hostel. It was a truly glorious few days with some terrific people. It is impossible to describe the beauty of the San Blas Islands in words. They are, without a doubt, a slice of Paradise!

29

PANAMA CITY / PANAMA CANAL

The hostel we were dropped off at in Panama City was really sweet (NOT!). I was booked into a twelve-bed dorm with extra air mattresses on the floor, so it was very cramped. Panama City itself was cool, though, and I had a fun night out on the town with people I met from the island trip. We hit a rooftop bar and a few other bars in the old city. I happened to run into an Aussie girl I had met months back in Bolivia, and we partied together since it was the last night of her six-month trip. It was a small world on the traveling circuit!

Panama City was by far the most Americanized city I had visited thus far on the trip. There were tall buildings and lots of chain stores, and the English language was much more prevalent. The city reminded me of Miami in some ways, yet not as rich and classy. My handy Lonely Planet informed me that the must-have local cuisine was ceviche and it could be had very cheaply. I treated myself several times to delicious $2.50 ceviche lunches at the local fish market.

As with every city I visited, I spent most of my days walking around exploring. While this city was more modern, spectacular historic churches and beautiful old buildings with cracked facades lined the streets as well. Harbors filled with both active and wrecked vessels encircled the city.

Of course, I had to pay a visit to the Panama Canal. I went to the Miraflores Locks, which were quite an engineering marvel to witness. My daytrip buddies and I were lucky enough to watch two massive ships passing through at the same time. It was viciously hot and sunny that day so the already slow process seemed to last forever as I balanced seeking out shade with seeing the locks do their magic. While I was generally very good about sun protection, I was well-sunburned by this point in the journey.

I was ready for some more remote, natural beauty and decided not to stay in Panama City for too long. My last day in Panama City concluded over a few $1.00 beers on the water with some new girlfriends. We engaged in priceless girl talk and discussed what 're-entry' into society would be like for all of us. Most people I met along my journey had anxiety about going home, and so did I!

Putting my angst aside, I decided that my next stop would be Santa Catalina, a remote surfing and diving village on the west coast of Panama. A lovely Aussie girl, Alyssa, that I had met during the San Blas boat trip and had been spending a lot of time with asked if she could tag along. She was a like-minded solo woman traveler who was traveling long term and winging it like me. Of course, I didn't mind having her join me, so we got ready to leave the big city.

30

SANTA CATALINA & BOQUETE, PANAMA

I t should come as no surprise by now that the logistics involved with getting to Santa Catalina were a bit tricky. From Panama City, Alyssa and I took a bus to a town called Sona, and then took a colectivo to the remote surfer and diver paradise called Santa Catalina on the west coast of Panama. We turned up with no reservations and easily found a hostel on the water for $12.00 a night, sharing a decent room with two twin beds.

Alyssa and I spent a few days in Santa Catalina hanging out on the beach and walking around town. I went diving one day near Isla Coiba in Coiba National Park, famous for its marine life. This was my first dive since my certification course so I was a bit apprehensive, but it was great! I saw lots of white tip reef sharks, a sea turtle, several huge eels, and many beautiful, brilliantly colored fish. The highlights of this dive included my first shark sighting and a seahorse sighting! It was very expensive, so it would be my last dive of the trip, but it was worth it.

Since the diving was expensive and I wanted to make the most of the rest of my trip, I decided to head to Boquete,

Panama next. Boquete is a mountainous jungle town located in the northern part of Panama between the east and west coasts. I booked a shuttle from Santa Catalina to Boquete and ended up missing the shuttle, as it left a half hour early. It was extremely strange that something was early in Latin America, and I had to stay an extra night in Santa Catalina until the next shuttle came. This wasn't the end of the world but was a bit annoying, as there was no WiFi in town and I had some research and planning to do. Making the most of it, I took in the sunset on the beach over a few beers with Alyssa.

As the shuttle rolled into Boquete, a rainbow shone over the lush jungle landscape. I was dropped off at a hostel where I inquired about availability. There were no rooms available on Night One, but they offered me the option to sleep in a tent on the property. I scoped it out and it was actually quite a nice little private tent so I took it. I would've stayed in the tent for a few days if it wasn't for the mold smell that permeated the space, but I moved inside once a bed became available.

I spent several days exploring the area. Boquete was named as one of the top places to retire in the world by AARP and because of this, the town was full of older Americans. It was actually quite bizarre, especially considering it was the first time during my trip that I was in a place with more than a handful of Americans around. Hearing the American accent had become a foreign thing to me at this point!

The town was populated with several very American supermarkets and cafés. One day, I visited a café where I was seated next to a table full of retired Texans conversing loudly in southern accents. At this café, I ordered a very American sandwich and it was delivered to me quickly. It felt like the twilight zone!

It was Superbowl season and it was easy to find a sports bar in this retirement haven. My home team, the New England Patriots, was playing so I watched the game at a sports bar with clientele that was made up primarily of Americans over the age of sixty-five. Sporting my Patriots hat, I rounded up a crew from the hostel and we watched the game (which of course, the Patriots won) over burgers and beers.

I spent one of my days in Boquete touring a coffee finca (farm) owned by a retired American guy who came to pick me up in his pickup truck. We walked through rows and rows of bushes where the beans were growing and drying on tarps in the sunlight. The farm was set among such a picturesque backdrop, with mountain views in every direction. I roasted my own coffee as part of the tour and I actually saved it until I returned home to Boston. Space in my bag was obviously limited but this coffee was the real deal, it was lightweight, and I was getting closer to the end of my travels so figured I could make it work.

Another day, I hiked the Sendero Quetzales trail with a German girl, Maya. I had met Maya previously in Santa Catalina, and ran into her at the hostel in Boquete. We set off for the trail, and as we walked by a farm on a dirt road, a baby lamb escaped under her barb-wired fence. She came 'baaa-ing' toward us, wanting to be pet and cuddled, which was insanely adorable. Then she followed us as we continued to walk down the road.

We named her Rose, and Rose wouldn't stop following us as we made our way to the trailhead. She was so little and unsteady on her feet that we became concerned about her. It didn't seem like she would be able to keep up with us for the entire hike or make it back to her farm on her own. Maya and I joked about how we might end up hiking up a muddy, slippery trail carrying a lamb for hours.

Fortunately, we came across some locals walking in the opposite direction and explained the situation to them. They picked up little Rose and carried her home. On the return trip from the hike, we paid her a visit. The adorable baby sheep was definitely the highlight of our hike.

The trail itself that day was a nice jungle trail, but was much more difficult than we expected! Maya and I hiked to a mirador (outlook), but were not able to see too much considering we were in a cloud forest. Hiking through the clouds was cool in and of itself though! We heard howling monkeys and saw some unique birds along the trail.

At one point, we heard a loud, scary grunt coming from the bushes which totally freaked us out. We froze, afraid to continue. Ultimately, we decided to clap and yell loudly to scare whatever it was away, which was probably a wild boar. It was a comical moment and thankfully, we bypassed the mystery animal without incident!

On the way down, I took a nasty spill, as the trail was very muddy and slippery. Slipping on a protruding root, I fell very hard onto my bum and onto that root, ending up with the most impressive bum bruise I had ever had. I could hardly sit down or sleep on my right side for a week!

It was quite chilly in the mountains of Boquete, so I decided to make a move to a beach. Next on my agenda was a visit to Bocas del Toro, Panama, where I would get some more warmth and sunshine in.

The final weeks of my trip were quickly approaching and I pondered my journey home. I was seriously considering finishing my trip with a cross country drive from California to Boston, something that had been on my bucket list for years. This would require a lot of planning in order to do it on the cheap—it is very expensive to rent cars, especially when you plan to drive them one way and over state lines. I decided to look into ride shares and the possibility of driving someone else's car.

The southern route appealed to me most, and I tentatively planned to drive from San Diego to the Grand Canyon to Austin, Texas to New Orleans, Louisiana, and then head north up the east coast. Via my blog, I reached out to see if anyone had any tips, places to stay, or knew anyone who needed a car driven from Point A to Point B. I also reached out to several close friends via email to see if anyone wanted to do all or part of the drive with me.

31

BOCAS DEL TORO & COSTA RICA

I n classic form, I arrived in Bocas del Toro fairly weary from the road. Bocas del Toro is an archipelago on the Caribbean coast of Panama. I checked into a hostel without doing much pounding of the pavement. The hostel seemed like it would suit my needs—it overlooked the water and was decorated with brightly colored and whimsical furnishings. One such furnishing was an old VW bus that had been turned into a bar. Colorful, retro lounge chairs were perched on a dock that hung over the ocean.

I met two American girls right off the bat and ended up spending a decent amount of time with them, island hopping and frequenting happy hours. It was easy to catch a boat to another island to visit different beaches. We would decide on where to go by referring to a map painted on a wooden plank in the center of town—very modern!

The island we were staying on had countless restaurants and bars. While the area was very touristy overall, the turquoise waters and white sand beaches were brilliant. Classic elephant-ear-shaped leaves on gnarled tropical tree branches dominated the coastline. There were plenty of photo ops involving a boat floating on its mooring in the distance in the dazzling waters. It was not uncommon to spot a sloth lazily climbing through the jungle.

The girls and I would set up shop on remote beaches and just relax, read, or chat all day. They found it funny that I used my scarf as a beach towel and were intrigued by my long-term trip and backpacking ways.

One of the women was a doctor and I consulted with her about something that was concerning me. A few lumps had developed in my armpit and I was afraid that something poisonous could have bitten me. She took a look and advised me to use hot compresses on them. I took her advice in a half-assed manner but the lumps did not seem to be going away. They were not very painful or large, so I decided to ignore my ailment for the time being, as I didn't want to deal with the travel insurance if I didn't have to.

While I enjoyed socializing with my new pals, I also needed to take some time to myself to contemplate my next and final moves as my trip was quickly coming to an end. I spent some time on the water which is where I am most content, taking leisurely walks along the beach or relaxing on a dock for hours on end. One day, I took a not-very-successful surf lesson. Another day, I rented a stand-up paddle board. I fell off the paddleboard at one point and my sunglasses sunk to the bottom of the ocean. Fortunately, the sunglasses were not expensive and $5.00 'Ray Bons' were easy to come by in those parts.

Speaking of losing things, I realized that I had left a bathing suit and a dress behind in Santa Catalina. These were big losses as my clothing situation was getting quite pathetic! However, I would be heading home soon. In fact, I had decided that Costa Rica would be my last stop and I would fly to California from there in mid-February to commence a cross country drive.

Bocas del Toro was a nice place, but too touristy for my liking. The American-like prices were a shock to the system as well, so I decided to head to the small town of Puerto Viejo, Costa Rica, a town I had visited in the past with friends on a short vacation. The border crossing to Costa Rica was another very interesting one. I had to go into several different buildings for various stamps and then walk over a rickety old train bridge. Once in Costa Rica, the road was blocked due to some kind of protest, so I had to walk along the main road for a while to get to my shuttle to Puerto Viejo.

When I first arrived in Puerto Viejo, I set up shop in a private room at a hostel on the outskirts of town for $19.00 per night. I realized quickly that this hostel was a little out of the way of the town center and best beaches, so I moved to a place called Hotel Puerto Viejo after one night. A fellow traveler told me that this place had private rooms for $12.00 each.

After a few days at Hotel Puerto Viejo, I gathered that it was a 'Hotel California' type of place, with a decent number of crackheads and weirdos lurking around. The room itself was also quite dark and depressing. The place did have some upsides, though. I met a Swedish woman, Lina, with whom I developed a fast friendship. She was hilarious, fun to be with, and strikingly beautiful.

Lina and I would drink cheap beer in what we referred to as 'the spot'—the front stoop of Hotel California. There was quite the rotation of characters revolving through the spot and we met one particularly memorable man who called himself Lefty. Lefty was missing his right arm, hence the nickname. Lina and I would smoke weed with Lefty and listen to crazy stories of his life experiences.

When we felt like classing it up a bit, Lina and I would go to a local bar or restaurant. We would chat about the struggles of life back home vs. the struggles of life on the road or just talk about men. It was nice to find people with whom I could relate and who could relate to me—people who were somewhat lost souls like myself.

Considering it was my last week in the tropics, I wanted to spend it in a tranquil place, so I moved out of Hotel California and into a yoga studio/hostel located on a very nice beach just down the road. I also rented a bike for the week, which became my primary mode of transport. The weather was on and off, and one day I rode the bike to a coffee shop in a torrential downpour!

Another day, I biked to my friend's vacation home in the area. I had visited this house while on a short holiday about seven years prior, and it was interesting to go back to check it out. The house was being rented at the time, otherwise I would've tried to stay there!

During the nicer days toward the end of my trip, I relaxed on the beautiful beaches and did some reading. I rented a surfboard one day and tried to practice what I had learned during my lesson in Panama. The surf was rough, though, and I was getting tossed around.

When I finally gave up and returned to my beach towel (or scarf, I should say!), a woman approached me and asked me if I thought it was worth it to rent a surfboard. This very pretty, older, hippie-ish woman named Karen said she had been watching me and the surfing looked challenging in the angry waters. I assured her that unless she was a seasoned surfer, she probably shouldn't bother wasting her money.

We got to chatting and it turned out she was from Santa Fe, New Mexico and was on a solo vacation for a couple of weeks. She had run into some trouble in San Jose when she first arrived in Costa Rica—after picking up her rental car, someone purposely hit her in traffic. This is a common scam that she was aware of so she turned around, brought the car right back to the rental agency, and decided to travel via bus.

I told Karen about my trip and we continued to have a nice conversation on the beach. We decided to meet up for dinner that night and we really hit it off. Karen told me that she would be taking a whitewater rafting trip to the airport when it was time for her to head back to the states, and suggested I join her. I was intrigued.

She told me that the itinerary involved the company picking you and your luggage up and driving you to the beginning of the whitewater adventure. They then take your luggage to the end of the route, while you spend the whole day rafting to that point. I inquired at the company's office in town and ended up signing up to take the same trip on the same day as Karen, as my flight was leaving the day after hers. I was confident that I could easily find a place to stay near the airport for one night.

Departure was fast approaching and during my last week in Costa Rica, I continued to soak it all up before the return to reality. I took the first yoga class I had taken in years. I ate lots of fresh fruits, especially mangoes. Socially, I went out for dinners and to several local hot spots with some people I had met on the shuttle from Panama.

I felt good in my fresh blue and white striped dress that Mia had loaned me when I saw her in Colombia. It's funny how your friend's used dress can be such a great wardrobe refresh! I was more tan and blonde than ever due to my over-exposure to the sun. I was also on the heavier side for me and was sporting a double chin, but frankly, I didn't really notice this at the time. Maybe it was the fact that I wasn't immersed in a society dominated by images of skinny celebrities and unrealistic pressures. Or maybe I was just fat and happy. Although, one day, I was reminded of the size of my ass as I was *walking* down the street and heard a local guy holler, "Do you have a license to drive that thing?" I burst out laughing.

My flight to California was booked for February 19th, 2015. Before embarking on my cross-country journey, I planned to spend a week visiting my brother in San Diego. My loose itinerary had me traveling by train from California to Flagstaff, Arizona to start the trip. I would stay in Flagstaff for a couple of days, exploring the Grand Canyon and Sedona. Then I would pick up a rental car and start driving east on Route 66!

Along the way, I knew I would visit Austin, where I would meet my best friend, Victoria, who would fly in from Boston. So, I had a deadline to meet in terms of my arrival to Austin. From there, Victoria and I would drive to New Orleans and Nashville together. We would fly home to Boston from Nashville in March.

The thought of winter back home sent a chill through my bones. Boston had been experiencing its snowiest winter in decades, getting a foot of snow every other day for a while. I kept hearing terms like 'ice dam' and 'snowpocalypse' when catching up with friends and family and I didn't like the sounds of these things!

It was incomprehensible that my trip was soon coming to an end and my emotions ran wild. On one hand, I was missing the comforts of home like clean, hot showers, food that wasn't deep fried, my own bed, a choice of outfits to wear, etc. On the other hand, I was very anxious about getting back to the grind, finding a new job, finding a new apartment, etc. My anxiety started to build to a point that I had not experienced in some time.

32

BACK ON US SOIL

When it was time to leave Costa Rica, I made my way to San Jose via whitewater raft as planned. The excursion was a lot of fun and I experienced my first Class Four rapids. Needless to say, I got completely soaked. Considering I was getting on a plane the following day, I had to pack up a bunch of wet clothes to bring with me to California. My sneakers needed to be tossed in the trash because they had no hope if I packed them wet.

I spent an uneventful night in a hostel in San Jose and flew to LAX the following day. At this point, I was starting to get pretty concerned about my armpit, which still had some questionable bumps in it. Since I would be back in the states in no time, though, I figured I could take care of any medical attention there if need be.

While my destination in California was San Diego, I flew into LAX as it was much cheaper. Some guys I met in Panama recommended the Pacific Surfliner train so I took that from LA to San Diego. It was a beautiful ride along the coast, with spectacular views of surfers bobbing in the waves and stunning homes dotting the mountains.

When I landed in Los Angeles, culture shock set in immediately. People stared at me schlepping my dirty backpacks around and I felt out of place. When I made a pitstop in the airport bathroom, I was astounded by its cleanliness. The littlest things came as surprises to me—toilet paper, soap, running water, and hand towels. Not to mention automatic flushing and dispensing! There were even hooks on the doors where I could hang my backpack and purse (not like there was any hope for my disgustingly filthy bags at that point after having rested them on countless grimy floors over the past six months).

Habits from the road stuck with me for a bit. I kept throwing toilet paper in the trash and it took me a while to get used to throwing it in the toilet again. Instinctively, I started speaking Spanish to the shuttle driver at the airport, asking him, "Cuanto tiempo a la estacion Union?" ("How long will it take to get to Union Station?"). This first American bus ride felt bizarre—I was able to ask a question in English, get an answer easily, and then arrive at my expected destination on time (via paved, smooth roads to boot)!

Curious people approached me and asked me questions, and I had some very amusing conversations upon my return to the states. My exchange with a traffic attendant at LAX went like this:

Traffic Attendant: Are you backpacking around the US?

Me: No, I am just returning from a backpacking trip through South and Central America. But I do plan to travel across the US now.

Traffic Attendant: Really?!?!

Me: Yes

Traffic Attendant: Woah, that's crazy! Did you, like, stay in hostels and stuff?

Me: Yes

Traffic Attendant: Woah! Isn't that dangerous?! Weren't you scared?!

Me: No

Etc., etc., etc.

When my brother picked me up from the train station in San Diego, part of our conversation went like this:

Brother: There is a hostel down the street and they have bunkbeds and stuff. Did you stay at places like that?

Me: Yes

Brother: Really?!?! I cannot picture that. Were people snoring?

Me: Yes and yes. I wore earplugs.

Etc., etc., etc.

In San Diego, I spent some time with my brother whom I had not seen in ages. We went bike riding, walked along the boardwalk, and just hung out while taking in views of the Pacific Ocean. I did lots of walking while visiting downtown San Diego, the Gaslamp Quarter, and Balboa Park for the first time. It felt good to get some exercise.

Coincidentally, Sofia, whom I had met months back during the Bolivian salt flats tour, was in San Diego at the same time as me! As you probably recall, we spent weeks together on and off in Bolivia, Peru, and Colombia and had really bonded during that time. The last I had seen of Sofia was when we said our goodbyes at the surf camp in Colombia as I rode off on a motorcycle taxi.

As fate would have it, our paths crossed again at the right place at the right time in San Diego. Sofia was couch surfing at the time and I was very fortunate to have her around as I encountered some family issues during my time in southern California. I never thought I'd find myself in San Diego being able to call a German friend that I met in Bolivia to meet me for emotional support. My spirits were lifted through hanging out with Sofia and her couchsurfing host, Justin.

They were empathetic, great listeners and they even invited me to a comedy show, which couldn't have come at a better time.

After spending a night on my brother's couch, I decided to move to a private room in a hostel to have my own space. En route to the hostel, while I navigated yet another public transport system, I was the recipient of an act of kindness that I had the opportunity to pay forward.

When I boarded a San Diego bus with all of my baggage, I presented the driver with a $5.00 bill for the $2.00 fare, but the driver did not have change. He advised me to ask some other passengers if they had change. I was totally haggard from schlepping my bags around in the heat. A very nice lady chimed in and offered me the $2.00 fare. I asked if she had change but she only had $2.00 and insisted I take it. Since the driver would not accept my $5.00, I had no other choice, so I took it and thanked her profusely. It was very kind of her and it made my day.

The following day, I was in a supermarket shopping for essentials for the next leg of my trip. An elderly Asian man who could not speak English was in front of me in the checkout line. His total came to $21.20 and he only had $20.00. Initially, he didn't understand that the cashier was telling him that he needed to put something back, but he ultimately proceeded to put back the last scanned item, a 12-pack of Bud Light. This was my chance to pay it forward! I chimed in "I can pay the $1.20." And that was that . . . it made me very happy.

This first visit to an American supermarket was full of other surprises. I easily acquired healthy food at the massive store filled with organized aisles. I also purchased familiar shampoo, conditioner, soap, vitamins, mascara, and peanut butter. The clerks were friendly and put my items into free bags. Finally, everything was so f*&king expensive!!!

Speaking of expensive, I finally made it to a doctor. The concerning lumps in my armpit were not improving and as I mentioned, I was afraid that something poisonous may have bitten me. So, I called the travel insurance company, they recommended a clinic, and I made an appointment. I had to pay upfront and then file a claim. There were no guarantees of coverage but ultimately, I got it reimbursed. The total cost for the doctor visit was $150.00. Welcome back to America!

I was diagnosed with a bacterial infection and I had to take antibiotics. The doctor, like the one I had met in Panama, told me to apply hot compresses to the area as much as possible. Considering I would be driving cross country and sitting in a car for about eight hours a day, this didn't seem very feasible. The doctor recommended I get hot water at my pitstops, which I did, and I was cured in no time.

The last day in San Diego was spent in last minute preparation mode for the next leg of my journey. Sofia and I both needed to pick up some essentials even though we were going in separate directions. I needed some warm clothing, closed toe shoes, underwear, and snacks for the long journey ahead, among other things.

We spent our last morning visiting my brother, having lunch, and walking the boardwalk on Pacific Beach. Then, we hit the downtown mall, which traumatized us with its very high prices. Luckily, we both found some great deals! We made compromises when it came to what we really wanted vs. what we really needed and could afford and carry on our journeys.

My shopping trip spoils included a pair of generic turquoise Keds from Forever 21 for $13.00 and a lightweight, packable down jacket from Macy's that I found on clearance for $26.00. Sofia and I joked about the trials and tribulations of trying to look pretty and fashionable on the road when you can carry so little, need versatile items, typically don't have access to things you need, and don't have a lot of money to spend.

Once the last-minute shopping was complete, we set off to catch our train. We would both be heading to LA to start our separate journeys so we had a bit more time left together. As we walked toward the train station fully loaded with backpacks and dressed in our eccentric travel outfits, we both caught a glimpse of ourselves in the window of a building and burst out laughing hysterically at the same time.

Aboard the Amtrak train bound for LA, we talked more about the impacts of travel on one's self—its effects on your confidence levels (in both directions), the emotions it elicits, and the unforgettable memories and experiences it brings that make everything worth it. We talked further about the qualities and skills someone needs to be able to travel long term—organization and logistical prowess, budgeting ability, social skills, expert communication skills, propensity to handle change, propensity to learn new languages and cultures, extreme flexibility and adaptability, empathy, people reading skills, an open mind, etc.

At one point, I got up from my seat on the train to retrieve my iPad charger from my large backpack. Three curious retirees struck up a conversation that went like this:

Curious Retirees: Excuse me, are you girls backpacking?!

Me: Haha, yes.

Curious Retirees: Really?!?!

Me: Yes.

Curious Retirees: Around the US?

Me: Now, yes, but for the last few months, South and Central America.

Curious Retirees: No way!!! By yourselves?!?

Me: Actually, we met along the way, so we were both solo at certain points, and together at others. I am from Boston and she is from Germany.

Curious Retirees: No way! That's crazy! So how do you do that? Do you plan it all in advance? Do you just wing it? Where do you stay? Aren't you afraid?! You must be really brave! That's the way to live! Wow!

Etc., etc., etc.

Sofia and I said 'goodbye for now' at Union Station in Los Angeles as I rushed off to catch the overnight train to Flagstaff, AZ. We laughed as the scent of the marijuana we had each acquired in San Diego permeated the air as we hugged.

I had booked a coach seat that did not recline much so was not able to get much rest on the train ride to Arizona. As I tried to settled in, I had a bit of a scare as I noticed police with K-9 dogs boarding the train a few cars ahead of mine. While I was sure these dogs were probably sniffing for bombs or huge piles of serious drugs, I felt paranoid about the pot stash in my backpack.

Thinking quickly, I ran down the small flight of stairs to the luggage area, removed the stash from my backpack, and simply placed it next to my backpack, out of sight of any passersby. The way I looked at it, it was no longer in my possession. Back at my seat, I waited anxiously as the dogs made their way through my train car without incident. Phew! Once I was confident the dogs were off the train and we were underway, I secured the stash back in my backpack.

Upon arrival in Flagstaff at 5:30 AM, it was seventeen degrees Fahrenheit, there was snow on the ground, and it was dark outside. After walking around somewhat lost for about twenty minutes, I arrived at the hostel to find that they did not leave the key in the mailbox as promised. I had a feeling that this would happen—typical travel snafu! This particular snafu was concerning though, based on the temperature outside and my lack of appropriate clothing. I was wearing my new down jacket, but no gloves or hat, and I was absolutely freezing.

A bit of panic set in as I recalled that the train station appeared to be closed and I needed some shelter. I walked back toward the station, hoping I could find some kind of 24-hour diner to shack up in for a few hours. Fortunately, I noticed the Amtrak ticket office was open and there were some benches in there. There were two other girls hanging out on the benches who appeared to be 20-something-year-old runaways.

I asked the guy at the counter if I could hang out for a few hours until my hostel opened and he joked that it was fine as long as I didn't cause any trouble. You could tell he liked the company of the ladies while working the graveyard shift. He asked what I was doing in Flagstaff and told me I looked like a 'river rafting person.' Ha!!! I blew up my inflatable pillow and half slept on a hard wooden bench while watching the Flagstaff morning news for two hours.

At 7:30 AM, I made my way back to the hostel and the door was still locked. I knocked and luckily, a maintenance guy came to the door. He told me that in order to check in, I actually had to go to the sister hostel a block away. More typical BS. I dropped my big bag and trekked over to the other place. After I explained the situation to the stoner at the front desk, he slowly but surely produced a key, apologized, and said I could have one night free. So, there was a silver lining after all . . .

Initially, I had the clean, nicely appointed ten-bed dorm room to myself and I took a nap until 11:00 AM. Then, I showered and walked to the visitor center in town to get some maps and figure out the best way to get to the Grand Canyon.

While downtown, I sauntered over to Budget Car Rental to inquire about rates, as the roundtrip shuttle to the Grand

Canyon cost over $50.00. The rental car would run me $37.00 and give me the flexibility to go at my own pace and stop wherever I wanted, so I decided to take it then and there. If I left right then, I would have enough time to drive to the Grand Canyon, explore a few different viewpoints, and make it to a very cool spot for sunset. So, I hopped on the road in my Oregon-plated Hyundai Accent.

Mind you, all mobile service was down in the state of AZ so I could not rely on my GPS (not like my sweet phone had reliable GPS in the first place). Thankfully, I had referred to enough maps to know the route I needed to take, and it was clearly signposted anyway. It felt very strange to be behind the wheel of a vehicle after six months! I was a little nervous at first, especially since I didn't purchase any additional insurance (my travel rewards credit card supposedly covered some kind of rental car stuff . . . I hoped it covered anything that may happen!).

I easily navigated to the Grand Canyon the old school way, bought a sandwich at the visitor center, and stopped at some lookout points. In the freezing cold, I watched the sun set from the Desert View Watchtower. It was glorious. Upon my request, some fellow tourists took a photo of me in my funny blue jacket and mismatched generic turquoise Keds. This photo is a truly comical memory of my first time at the Grand Canyon.

The following day, I had the rental car until 2:00 PM, so I got an early start on a drive to Sedona. I drove through beautiful Oak Creek Canyon and explored Red Rock National Park. In downtown Sedona, I popped into some shops to check out the gypsy wares and even had a tarot card reading . . . when in Rome!

During my final day in Flagstaff, I prepared for the next part of my journey. While sitting in a trendy coffee shop on Route 66, I did some research. I had taken a handy AAA

Arizona/New Mexico tour book from the hostel which included great maps and information. My plan was to wing it to a significant degree, but my route would be straightforward enough.

Basically, I planned to drive east on Route 66 until I hit Albuquerque. Along the way, I would stop to visit the Painted Desert and Petrified Forest. I was not sure about my next lodging situation, but there seemed to be a plethora of places along Route 66, so I didn't concern myself with booking anything in advance.

Once my research was complete, I did a little shopping. I wanted to check out the cute shops in downtown Flagstaff before departing. I was also in the market for an AUX cord and a CD or two so that I would have something more than fuzzy radio stations to listen to during my long drive. During my shopping trip, I had yet another amusing conversation, this time with a girl working at a jewelry store in Flagstaff. It went like this:

Girl: Are you visiting Flagstaff?

Me: Yes, I'm just passing through for a few days.

Girl: Oh, that's great. Where have your travels taken you?

Me: I am on a cross-country trip now and I just got back from backpacking through South America.

Girl: No way! I've always wanted to go to that country. Isn't it dangerous??

During this shopping trip, I was not able to locate an AUX cord, but I did purchase a CD for the first time in about fourteen years. There was no way I could be stuck on the open road without tunes! The CD I chose was Blake Shelton and I chose it for a few reasons—it was $9.99, it had several excellent love ballads I could sing along to, and I figured country was the way to go while driving through the southwest. I ended up leaving it in the rental car accidentally but it got a lot of airtime on that first leg of my drive!

It was time to set off for New Mexico! As I always did before I made a move, I reflected on where I was both literally and figuratively. An important lesson I had learned while traveling was simply that some things never change. Specifically, I realized that I was still Type-A and impatient to some degree and probably always would be. My patience had improved by leaps and bounds out of necessity, but patience is not a quality inherent in my DNA, and it was something I would need to consciously work on.

Perhaps more importantly, my reflections shifted to the fact that I was feeling a bit depressed since returning to the states. It is normal to feel this way after returning home from long term travel and I had read a number of articles about it. However, the reality of my trip coming to a close was starting to really set in, and it made me very anxious! I needed to start thinking about finding a job, a place to live, etc., etc.

All of these thoughts ran through my mind as I began to navigate through a snowy, cold winter which I was not yet accustomed to. As usual, I tried to set any negativity aside and focus on enjoying the homestretch of my trip.

33

ROAD TRIP - AZ / NM / TX

Bright and early one morning during a lovely winter storm, I left Flagstaff. I had called a taxi to pick me up at 8:15 AM from my hostel and bring me to the airport where I would pick up a rental car. Lucky for me, as I was having breakfast and chatting with my new roommate, she offered to drive me to the airport on her way to a workshop in Sedona. So, I cancelled the taxi and saved myself $15.00. Score!

The drive to the airport was not pretty . . . icy roads and icy precipitation. I was nervous about the first leg of the drive, but knew the storm would wane as I drove further east.

At the airport, I picked up my sweet Toyota Yaris and started heading east on Route 40, which is at times Historic Route 66, and at times, straight highway. The beginning of the drive was horrific, as the highway was full of tractor trailers, ice, and slush. It was a white-knuckle drive in a compact vehicle for about an hour but then it got much better.

I executed my planned detour through the Petrified National Forest and the Painted Desert. These places were very nice and didn't take me too out of the way. The scenery on Day One of the cross-country drive was striking—lots of mountains and red rock formations. It was like driving on the moon and was actually very similar to Valle de la Luna in Chile that I had visited during my recent travels. The drive also took me by several classic Southwestern storefronts complete with copper cowboys and covered wagons. A highlight for me was seeing tumbleweeds literally blowing across the highway! Classic!

While I was jamming out to Blake Shelton, I debated on whether to conclude Day One's drive in Albuquerque or to continue on further to Santa Fe that day. Santa Fe would involve an extra hour or so of driving and was forecasted to get more snow, so I decided to sleep in Albuquerque for a night. During that first day of driving, I drove for a total of about five or six hours and with breaks, I was on the road for seven hours.

The driving wasn't bad at all once the storm was behind me. I actually enjoyed being back behind the wheel, singing out loud, and taking in the sights on the open road. My breaks included a very short hike in the Petrified National Forest (it was freezing and windy), a Wendy's lunch break, and of course a few bathroom stops. I had not eaten fast food in years and I did not feel very well after the Wendy's break. However, I wanted something quick and the options on that stretch of road were slim to none (i.e. Wendy's, McDonald's, and horrible looking trucker shacks).

Upon arrival to Albuquerque, I cruised by the Route 66 hostel, which I had heard about from someone I met at the hostel in Arizona. The guy who mentioned it described the place as 'not very clean' and considering he was not very clean himself, I figured the place would be a dump. It was. So, I utilized my handy AAA tour book (what am I ninety years old?!?) to find a place to stay and decided on the AAA-recommended EconoLodge.

Back in my old life, I would have considered this to be a dump, and it looked like one from the outside. However, the interior of the room was a pleasant surprise, with nice new beds, modern décor, and a flat screen TV. It was my most expensive night of lodging yet at $66.00. After sitting in the car all day long, it was worth it, though! I was exhausted and ready to do absolutely nothing, but I did need to feed myself.

I walked around the Nob Hill area near the university which was a trendy area with loads of restaurants. Ultimately, I opted out of eating dinner at one of these restaurants as the Wendy's was still sitting heavy in my stomach and I was totally beat. Instead, I grabbed some popcorn at Walgreen's, went back to my comfy hotel room, and watched The Notebook for what was probably the twentieth time. It was awesome.

I also called my new friend Karen, the Santa Fe resident whom I met in Costa Rica, and told her that I was in Albuquerque. She invited me to spend the night at her place the following night and I accepted. I had heard that Santa Fe was much cooler than Albuquerque and I figured it would be nice to get some human interaction in with a very nice woman I met on my trip. As I mentioned, Karen was a very pretty, I would estimate 50-ish-years-old, free spirited, hippie-in-a-good-way lady. She had to work at her massage studio until 3:00 PM the next day, so I decided to explore both Albuquerque and Santa Fe during the day and then meet up with her in the evening.

The following morning, I ate the crappy breakfast at the hotel, indulging in a mini cinnamon roll and some raisin bran, and then drove to the Old Town area of Albuquerque to walk around. It was a very charming area filled with touristy shops and galleries. Next, I stopped by the top-rated bakery in town to get a coffee for the road and sample the free New Mexico State cookie that I learned about on Yelp.

From there, I drove for one hour to Santa Fe. I yelped 'authentic New Mexican food' in Santa Fe, so had a destination to plug into the GPS for my lunchtime arrival. My lunch was delicious—a typical New Mexican meal of pork marinated in classic red chile sauce (NM is all about their red and green chiles!), rice, and beans. After lunch, I parked in the center of town near the main plaza and walked around exploring shops and galleries. There were so many wonderful galleries in Santa Fe and the adobe-dominated architecture throughout the city was remarkable.

When Karen finished work, she called to give me directions to her beautiful home in the foothills of Santa Fe. I wrote them down, as she informed me that the GPS would not work out there. So as not to show up empty handed, I stopped at a liquor store and found a bottle of wine from a vineyard that I had actually visited in Argentina.

While I found Karen's street easily, I had a lot of trouble finding the house. It was located on a long, dirt, hilly road with some lingering ice and snow, and most houses had long driveways without clearly posted numbers. Finally, after going up and down the road twice, I thought I discovered her driveway. Wondering if I was in the right place, I heard Karen call out, "Kerie!" as I creeped around her property.

Her home was a beautiful, traditional structure that she had built to her specifications. She cooked some delicious enchiladas with homemade green chile sauce, and her sister and brother-in-law came over to dine with us. We all drank wine, chatted, and had a very nice time. When her sister and brother-in-law left, Karen and I hopped into her outdoor hot tub, set among the beautiful desert hills with spectacular views of the stars.

Finally, I went to sleep on Karen's Tempurpedic pull out sofa which was incredibly comfortable. I woke up to an array of beautiful New Mexican birds perched on the bird feeders just outside my window, and Karen cooked us a breakfast of farm fresh eggs and leftover enchiladas. It was glorious.

After breakfast that morning, I thanked Karen for her hospitality and left Santa Fe to start the 4-hour-ish journey to Amarillo, Texas. I decided the 'tourist sight of the day' would be Cadillac Ranch, a roadside attraction consisting of several brightly colored Cadillacs buried upside down in a row. I ate Subway on the road (a little better than Wendy's, but still gross in my opinion), and stopped off to take a few photos of the half-buried Cadillacs. It was not as much of a tourist sight as I had anticipated. There were a few people pulled over on the highway frontage road checking out the old Cadillacs that were actually pretty far away.

Needless to say, I didn't stay long and continued on my journey. The police pulled me over shortly after entering Texas. Apparently, I was driving 85 miles per hour in a 75 miles per hour area, which is not surprising as I've always had a lead foot. In fact, I was lucky they only clocked me at 85 mph. The cop was very nice and I only received a written warning. Phew!

Next on the agenda was locating the Greyhound bus station in Amarillo while there was still daylight, as I was scheduled to depart the following morning at 6:00 AM on a 12-hour bus ride to Austin, Texas. Once I located the station, I needed to find a place to stay nearby. Rolling into Amarillo, I easily located the bus station and scoped out the immediate area for lodging.

The only hotel nearby seemed to be the Marriott Court-yard so I stopped in and inquired about the rates. With a AAA discount, it was $125.00 a night. I asked if they had an airport shuttle as I needed to return my rental car to the airport. They said no, and had no idea how much a taxi would cost. Hertz, the rental car company, also had no information regarding shuttles, pick-up services, or taxi rates when I called them to inquire. I couldn't justify spending $125.00 on one night of lodging, especially if there was no airport shuttle included, so I asked the guy at the front desk if there were any other hotels in the area.

He informed me that there was a place called the Civic Center Inn a block away and that it was much cheaper. I asked him if it was a dump and he said, "Well, it's . . . vintage." I told him I would check it out and maybe return if it was awful.

The Civic Center Inn was, in fact, quite 'vintage,' but it was also $45.00 a night, so . . . I'll take it! Since I had the rental car until 10:00 PM if I wanted it, I didn't have to spend any time in the crappy room and was able to do a little more sightseeing during the afternoon. I dropped my bags in the not-so-bad but not-so-nice room, and decided to hit up the Big Texan.

The Big Texan is a restaurant (or institution if you will) where if you eat a 72 oz. steak in under an hour, it's free. I did not attempt this feat, but the place itself was really cool to visit, with lots of vintage Route 66 memorabilia adorning the walls and for sale in the gift shop. The bar wasn't very inviting and the general seating area was very family oriented, so I decided not to eat there. Plus, I had spotted a Buffalo Wild Wings nearby that would be much more conducive to a single person eating at the bar. I had never been to a Buffalo Wild Wings, so why not?!

With plenty of time to kill, I ate some wings, drank a beer, returned the rental car, and got a taxi back to downtown Amarillo. I returned to the Bates Motel, I mean Civic Center Inn, and tried to catch up with my blog which was a task that had become increasingly difficult as time passed.

Thinking forward to the next day, I hoped that my Greyhound experience would be better than some of the South American bus experiences I had encountered, but I knew not to get my hopes up. At least I would get a break from driving before meeting up with Victoria, which I was really looking forward to. Victoria and I would be doing a lot of driving together (and I'm sure a lot of partying) so I figured it would be nice to rest for a bit.

My bus would arrive in Austin one day before Victoria's flight, and I would be awaiting her arrival with bells on! I booked us into a very trendy, highly-rated, well-located hostel. It would be Victoria's first experience in a hostel and I was glad that she was willing to give it a go. I was also scared of how she might react as she likes the finer things in life! While Victoria had agreed to stay in hostels in Austin and Nashville, she insisted upon a Marriott in New Orleans, which I agreed to, especially because she treated!

The next day, my high hopes for the Greyhound experience were shattered when the filthy bus departed an hour late and we then proceeded to pick up several freshly released convicts from a Texas state prison. I was sleeping when we picked them up, but when I woke up, the nice guy sitting next to me informed me of the situation. At first, I thought he was messing with me, but then I took a look around.

There were several men with large manila envelopes which I could only presume contained their personal belongings. I overheard a man asking a fellow passenger if he could borrow his phone to make a call. The passenger obliged and the man called who I presumed to be a former boss, arranging to start work right away. The whole situation made me sad. I did not feel threatened by any of these folks, but I also had no clue what they were in for. For the duration of the trip, I continued to mind my business and swore off busses for a while.

34

ROAD TRIP - AUSTIN / NEW ORLEANS / NASHVILLE

When I arrived in Austin, I checked into the hostel, dropped my bags in the room, and made my way to the lounge that was hidden behind a secret revolving bookshelf door. The lounge was extremely charming and I knew Victoria would like it. However, the room where we would be sleeping was crowded and messy which was kind of a bummer because I wanted her first impression of hostels to be favorable. Oh well!

The next day, I waited outside of the hostel for Victoria's taxi to arrive. It was super exciting to see one another after almost six months and we gave each other big hugs in the street. Leading the way to our humble abode, I warned her about the situation and reminded her that it was only for a night or two and we would be drunk anyway by the time we got 'home.' I had advised her in advance that ear plugs and an eye mask would be critical items for her packing list and she was prepared with those (years later, she still uses these items all the time).

It was funny to observe my friend as she observed the surroundings. She was a great sport but I could tell she was not thrilled about the accommodations. We decided to get right down to business—freshening up and going out to hit the town. The communal bathroom situation was not ideal, but we had some serious laughs (mostly at my expense) as we got ready for the evening.

Victoria asked me, "Are you really gonna wear that?" expressing her horror over my choice of outfit. I had very limited clothing at that point and also didn't give much of a f#@k, but we cracked up laughing over my outfit nonetheless. I was wearing black leggings, a purple floral tank top, and a camo jacket. My hair had grown obscenely long and I guess I must have looked a little whacky. I confirmed that yes, I was going to wear that particular outfit, and we finished our preparations.

Before heading out, Victoria gave me a special gift—several fresh pairs of undies from Victoria's Secret. Score!!! She had also done me a solid by digging through my frenetically packed boxes in her basement to find me a pair of jeans and a sweater. I looked forward to donning some fresh duds on our next night out.

Our next order of business was locating a bar, which was not challenging considering our hostel was very conveniently located. We were in search of a place where we could sit outside and enjoy the seasonable weather that Austin had to offer in March. We quickly found a suitable spot and sat on a second-floor balcony where we started to catch up over some beers.

Because we were the only ones on the balcony, the waitress would go up and down a flight of stairs to tend to us and only come around when she knew we probably needed a fresh beer. This worked out perfectly for us, as we were able to get away with smoking a joint up there unbeknownst to the staff. We were literally crying laughing as I whipped out the stinky, triple-bagged stash that I had brought from California. The doubled-over laughs continued as I relayed the story of how I thought the dogs were going to find it on the Amtrak train.

More fun ensued as we bar-hopped around Austin. At one point, as we were crossing the street, I slipped and fell, losing a shoe in the process. A man in a cowboy hat helped me up, picked up my shoe, and put it back on my foot like Cinderella as Victoria died laughing. A trip to Austin wouldn't be complete without eating some delicious BBQ so we indulged at a local favorite spot.

During the following day, we walked around town to take in some sights and shop for cheap cowboy hats for our cross-country drive. As I've mentioned, walking is my preferred method of transportation when exploring new cities, but not everyone shares this preference. Victoria still jokes with me to this day that I am 'that friend who says it's not far but then we walk for miles to get there.'

When it was time to leave Austin, we picked up a rental car and set off for New Orleans, donning our new cowboy hats for the ride. The plan was to switch off driving to share the burden. Victoria needed to get some work done, so I drove the morning shift while she worked from the passenger seat. Using trusty Yelp, we located a great Tex Mex place in Houston for a lunchtime pitstop.

From there, Victoria took over and we belted out tunes as we made our way along the open road. Our playlist can only be described as diverse and excellent. Classic gangsta rap (with me performing Snoop Dogg's parts and Victoria doing Dr. Dre's parts) were followed by country ballads, old school R&B (KC and Jo Jo, anyone?), and the latest Top 40.

During the drive, it became clear that my brain did not seem to be firing on all cylinders. As we rolled into Houston, I commented, "Welcome to Dallas!" At another point, I remarked on how Nate Dogg is the 'Queen of Hooks' instead of what I meant to say, the 'King of Hooks.' These slips, among others, led Victoria and I to determine that I had a screw loose from being away for so long! Victoria told me that I should do some brain teasers as we cackled over my ridiculousness.

The end of Day One's drive led us into New Orleans as planned. We checked into the Marriott and dropped off the rental car. For the next couple of days, we wouldn't need a car and it was cheaper to rent them in separate legs anyway. With our priorities in line, we freshened up in the luxurious Marriott facilities and hit Bourbon Street, where we grabbed some grenades to begin the evening. Popping in and out of different venues, we took in some live music and talked to random strangers.

When hunger hit, we grabbed fried chicken from Willie's Chicken Shack and brought it back to the hotel room where we chowed it down after smoking a joint. For our classy fried chicken hotel room dinner, we donned our cowboy hats and laughed and laughed. Hitting the streets again, this time heavily under the influence, we felt like salmon swimming upstream among the crowd.

The following day, we explored more of the city (on foot of course), but first indulged in a delicious brunch. We had Bloody Mary's and mimosas for a little hair of the dog and then walked around the Garden District and scoped out the shoreline. Finally, we went on a mission to find a crawfish meal, which was more challenging than expected, but ultimately successful. Victoria became slightly annoyed with me because I was on such a tight budget and I complained about the cost of everything. Aside from that, though, our little road trip was progressing swimmingly.

After one more night on the town in New Orleans, we grabbed another rental car and set off for Nashville. Obviously, we sang our hearts out to our epic soundtrack along the way. Upon arrival to Nashville, we checked into our hostel which we were pleasantly surprised with. The ten-bed dorm room was all ours with the exception of one other girl. The room, bathroom, and hostel itself were cleaner and more spacious than the place in Austin. Victoria seemed relieved which in turn provided me with a sense of relief.

Surprise, surprise—we freshened up and went out drinking. The bars of Broadway lured us in with their country music, dancing, and merriment. The people watching (a favorite hobby of mine) was fantastic and we observed some very serious country line dancers in addition to revelers on bachelor and bachelorette parties. A night of bar hopping ensued and we slept in the next morning in our quiet, almost private room. Figuring we should be somewhat responsible adults and do some sightseeing, we visited the Country Music Hall of Fame once we dragged ourselves out of bed.

Night Two involved much of the same debauchery as Night One. Before we headed out, I finally ditched the brown flats that had been my primary 'fancy' footwear for ages. Let's just say they had more than seen their day. Victoria spotted them in the bin and proclaimed, "Thank God you finally got rid of those things!!" as we howled with laughter.

The VERY SAD day finally came when it was time to go home. Victoria and I flew to Boston from Nashville and her husband picked us up at Logan Airport. I was taken aback by the sheer convenience of the airport pickup—someone I knew picking me up in a personal vehicle as opposed to figuring out how to get to my destination via public transport.

It was surreal to be back in Boston. As we drove, I noticed new buildings that had popped up behind the walls of snow that lined the highway. I felt a sense of tingly anticipation as I contemplated the next phase of my life, especially knowing that I couldn't put it off any longer. What was next for me?

EPILOGUE

Upon my return to Boston, I stayed with Victoria and Kyle for a week or two. Soon after my homecoming, Victoria walked into the kitchen one day to discover me crying over my eggs. I felt very confused and lost—I didn't know what I wanted next and what steps I needed to take to get to this illusory destination. As though my looming major life decisions didn't put enough on my plate, I also felt very isolated in the suburbs without a car.

It didn't take long for me to move into my friend Mia's small one-bedroom apartment in South Boston with her. At first, I just plopped an air mattress down in the living room. Mia wanted to move out of the apartment eventually and she was trying to save money, so we shared the place for a while. People thought I was nuts because I stayed on a mattress in the living room (I eventually moved my real mattress into the living room to replace the air mattress). Little did they know, this was luxury compared to where I had been shacking up.

Ideally, I wanted to take the apartment over from Mia, but I wouldn't be able to afford it without a decent job. I commenced my job hunt, utilizing recruiters to help me find something that might be a good fit. The job hunt was not exciting and it was freezing and very snowy in Boston. Mia, like Victoria, soon discovered that I was totally depressed and prone to crying at the drop of a dime. Being back in a big American city even led me to start feeling self-conscious about my weight—much more so than when I was away.

Ultimately, I secured a finance position with a higher education institution in the area. This was not as 'corporate' as my prior roles and I felt like it had more of a purpose. Once I landed the job, Mia and I discussed turning over the apartment. She wasn't ready to move out, but she wanted to save even more money, so we traded the bedroom for the living room mattress for a while. I moved up in the world to my very own private bedroom, while she crashed in the living room for a period of time, paying less, of course, while banking some cash.

Once Mia had her transition plan in place, we arranged for me to take over the apartment officially with the landlord. I was the third person in our friend group to rent this apartment, and he was totally fine with it. He was none too happy that two of us had been living there for a while, though, which he had figured out from observing the water usage. However, he just made us give him a little extra cash to cover that.

I started my new job in June, three months after my return to Boston. Because I was gainfully employed before my close friend Grace's wedding festivities, I considered rejoining the wedding party. However, I didn't think it was very classy to invite myself back into the mix so I wasn't too sure how to handle the situation. Tragically, during that time, Grace's mother passed away. As we gathered to mourn her loss, we all felt closer than ever and Grace's husband, Thomas, suggested I participate in the wedding after all. Of course, I agreed and was very glad to be involved again, although I wished the circumstances were different.

While I tried to last as long as possible without a car, I ultimately purchased a very reasonable and modest used vehicle, a departure from my prior propensity to lease brand new vehicles. I was content with my new job and apartment for some time. Eventually, I made several major life changes yet again, but those are topics for another day!

That September, I met Sofia and Zoe in Munich for Oktoberfest. Sofia hosted us and we had an absolutely magnificent reunion. When we showed up to her downtown flat, her front door was decorated with the following message: "Welcome South America's Best Threesome!" The letters were cut out of traditional blue and white checkered patterned paper. Upon entering the flat, there were large, soft Bavarian pretzels and huge mugs for beer awaiting us. Sofia loaned us her extra, genuine dirndls and lederhosen and we all dressed up and had a grand time visiting the different beer tents. These girls and I keep in touch to this day and I believe we always will.

My sabbatical was such a defining experience and fundamentally changed me. Most importantly, I appreciate the small things now more than ever. I am satisfied and feel as though I have 'enough.' I don't strive to keep up with the Joneses and I am totally at peace with that. I do my best to be a good person, citizen, and steward of the environment so that our beautiful world can continue to prosper in the future.

In closing, I share some irony. Six years after my trip, my large backpack was stolen out of my locked storage unit in Newton, MA, named one of the 'safest cities in America.' I can't help but think of all the folks who asked me about my journey, "But isn't that dangerous?!?!"

APPENDIX A: SAFETY TIPS

- Don't walk down dark alleys
- Carry a small flashlight just in case
- Don't get drunk or high alone or with people you don't trust or know very well
- Always be aware of your surroundings
- Wear a money belt to store your passport, cash, and any other valuables
- Do not flaunt valuables like expensive jewelry, clothes, or handbags
- For women, it can be helpful to wear a fake wedding ring. This can sometimes deter unwanted advances
- Research common scams in areas you will be visiting so you will be prepared if one of them happens to you
- Know where you are going and how you will get back if you are going out at night
- Be sure to use old school navigation tools as backup to modern instruments (google useful maps while you have WiFi and take screenshots so

you have them accessible at any time you need them)

- Make a fake phone call from a taxi if needed, saying "I'll be there in X number of minutes" so the taxi driver thinks someone is expecting you
- Let people know about your plans whenever possible

APPENDIX B: BUDGETING TIPS

Listed below are the steps I took in coming up with a savings plan to travel:

Make a list of all of your expenses.

Put them into categories that completely separate necessary, unavoidable expenses (such as rent and food) from those that are discretionary (dinner out, manicures, new clothes). Identify where you can cut costs from the discretionary expenses. This is the hard part because you obviously don't want to make cuts to things that make you happy.

For example, all of my discretionary income went to what I broadly categorized as 'entertainment.' Going out for food and drinks in the city, weekends away, golf tournaments, manicures, Uber and cab rides home after nights out on the town that had already broken the bank, etc. All of these things made me happy, so it was difficult to think about sacrificing them.

However, you don't need to sacrifice everything—you just need to be more selective about where you spend your money. Perhaps most importantly, always keep the end game in mind when you are considering making a foolish expenditure. Think, "Would I rather have this immediate gratification, or would I rather bank this money to make my upcoming adventure even more awesome?"

I realize this is very difficult and in fact, I found it painful. But it can be done, and it needs to be done if you want to execute your own austerity plan. If you must go on that ski weekend or beach weekend, buy food and booze for the house instead of going out. This can save hundreds of dollars in no time!

Other examples of areas where you can cut costs:

- Bring lunch to work as opposed to buying it. I know you've heard this one a million times, but that's because it works!
- Cook at home or go to a friends' place for dinner instead of dining out. A glass of wine with dinner costs $10.00+ if you go out . . . a whole bottle costs $10.00 if you stay in!
- Look for deals! Why spend $15.00 on a martini on a Friday night when you can seek out $1.00 drafts? Why eat at an expensive place when there is a decent place that has a great special going?
- Cancel your gym membership and commit to working out outside or in your living room
- Cancel your cable and/or any excess television services and subscriptions
- Cancel any unnecessary music subscriptions
- Don't buy new clothes for the current season. Mix

and match what you already have, and only allow yourself to purchase key items that can be taken on your trip (i.e. quick dry, comfortable, versatile clothing)

You've probably heard plenty of these before, but you'd be surprised at how quickly your savings will add up if you actually execute and make the sacrifices. I sacrificed bachelorette parties, weekends away on the beach, fun nights out on the town, etc. but it was all worth it when I was able to travel with the money I saved.

Evaluate your current living situation.

Can you move to a cheaper, or even free, place (like a family member's or friend's home) to save money for a while? Is it possible to get out of your apartment lease early or sell your home? Can you sublet?

Sell things on eBay or Craigslist.

Take a look around your living space and sell anything that you don't truly need. This is easier than you might think. Here are some examples of things I sold:

- Old backpack for $25.00
- Pair of eyeglasses I would never wear again for $20.00
- One-piece ski suit for $35.00
- Air conditioner for $60.00
- Rollerblades for $50.00

These small sums add up! I did not sell my furniture or TV, as I would need these things upon my return, but these are great things to sell if you are traveling long term. I stored my furniture in my friend's basement. I got rid of my leased car by finding a dealer that would take it off my hands with no penalties.

Use a credit card with a rewards system to pay for everything.

I started to pay for absolutely everything with a credit card that earned points that could be used toward travel-related expenses. I paid it off immediately every month in order to avoid interest charges, while still accruing points. I planned to use my accumulated points to pay for lodging, transport, etc. during my trip. It is important to get a credit card with no foreign transaction fees if your travels will take you abroad!

APPENDIX C: PREPARING TO TRAVEL LONG-TERM

Vaccinations

There are a number of vaccinations that are recommended for travel to certain countries. Checking www.cdc.gov is a great place to start to gain an understanding of the vaccinations you may need. It is important to get an immunization history from your doctor so you can compare what you need to what you have already received.

Next, schedule an appointment at a travel clinic to start the process of getting vaccinated, as this can take a while due to shots that are part of a series. Many doctor's offices have travel clinics, and if not, your doctor should be able to recommend one. While some vaccinations are required for entry to certain countries, others are optional. Furthermore, insurance may not cover immunizations that are considered 'travel-related.' It is important to understand what your insurance company will cover before deciding which vaccines to get. Below is a list of the vaccinations I received and why:

- Yellow Fever: Imperative—a certification of this one was required to enter certain countries. I received a bright yellow, greeting card shaped certificate for this, which I put into my pile of 'very important things to pack.

- Hepatitis A/B: Hepatitis B is a standard vaccination and most people have probably had it. However, Hepatitis A is considered 'travel-related.' Because I had not finished my Hepatitis B series, I was able to get a Hepatitis A/B combo series. This involves three shots over a period of about one month, so you need to plan accordingly to ensure you can complete these prior to departure. This was a highly recommended vaccine and one that I easily decided to get.

- Rabies: This is an optional three shot series. I had a tough time deciding on this one. My friend who had recently traveled long term in Asia did not get it and discouraged me a bit. There was also a chance that it wouldn't be covered by my insurance and would cost around $800.00. I considered the chances of getting attacked by a rabid dog or bat and unfortunately, deemed those chances to be pretty decent.

Here's why—I was bitten by a wild monkey in Bali during a vacation, which was terrifying (but apparently one of the most hilarious moments my friends had ever witnessed). On the same trip, my friend was chased by a pack of stray dogs. Based on these experiences, I thought I better get the vaccine. To make matters more confusing, though, I heard that if you were to get bitten by a rabid animal, the vaccine doesn't help you much and you still need to receive painful treatment. In the end, I believe I opted out of this one, but I honestly cannot recall for sure at the time of this writing!

- Typhoid: This can be a shot or an oral vaccine. It is highly recommended for most of the countries I was planning to visit, and I had heard a few stories about friends of friends getting typhoid. Not something I wanted to deal with on the road, so I opted for the oral vaccine (did I mention I was a wimp about needles?!). The oral vaccine needed to be taken on an empty stomach in the morning for four consecutive days and you are not supposed to eat for an hour after taking it. As someone who eats breakfast the moment I wake up, I found it challenging to determine when I would be able to forgo an early breakfast for four days in a row, but I made it happen in the name of wanderlust!

In addition to the above vaccines, I also received medication for traveler's diarrhea, altitude sickness, and malaria to take along with me.

Telephone & Communication

WhatsApp is one of the best methods to communicate with new travel buddies and people back home. Facetime, email, and social media are also great communication tools. Clearly, you need access to the internet to use these apps, so try to make all of your plans and do all of your touching base while you have that access.

You can also buy SIM cards in the countries you visit and put them into a phone that is GSM capable and unlocked (you can find a smartphone on Amazon that has these qualities), but this is not totally necessary. Personally, I purchased a smartphone that would be compatible with T-Mobile in the USA since I needed a phone before and after my trip. I also brought an iPad.

Insurance

Travel insurance is very important. I chose to get travel insurance through an organization called World Nomads based on recommendations from friends. For starters, I purchased a four-month package at a cost of $350.00. This insurance company allowed you to add time to the policy at any point which was convenient considering the timeline of my trip was still up in the air. Travel insurance is a must and yes, I did use it for an infection I acquired toward the end of my trip in Costa Rica!

Country research

It is important to do some research on the places you will be traveling to—you should at least acquire a general understanding of the culture, weather, political situation, economy, etc. The website www.travel.state.gov provides great information on entry/exit requirements, embassies, and potential dangers. Keep a small journal of critical information such as this. Note I said 'small' journal—when traveling long term, it's important to minimize bulk and weight wherever you can!

It is also important to research what the weather will be like during the times you plan to be in certain regions. This was challenging for me, as I intended to 'wing it' to a great extent, so couldn't predict exactly where I would be and when. That said, I researched the general weather patterns during the general times I planned to be in certain places so that I knew what to pack for clothing.

Accommodations

Research potential accommodations ahead of time. Pounding the pavement is a great alternative to booking everything ahead of time, but it is useful to book lodging for at least a night or two so that you have a destination upon arrival in a new place.

It is always prudent to have a backup plan. In addition to the standard hostel option, there are all kinds of lodging alternatives available in today's day and age. Couchsurfing and homestays are great options especially if you want to get immersed in the culture. Finally, talking to and learning from other travelers along the way is one of the best ways to find your ideal accommodations.

Things to Pack/Bring

Bring as little as possible in order to lighten your load, but make sure you have enough to live on for the duration of your trip. I traveled with a large, typical 'backpacker's backpack' and a smaller, regular sized backpack as my luggage. Below, I've listed some useful items when it comes to packing for a long-term trip. What you bring will of course depend on your destination(s).

- Sport/waterproof/sweatproof sunscreen.
- Deet (at least 30%) or picaridin (at least 20%) bug spray.
- Ibuprofen and any necessary prescription medications.
- Quick dry towels—one normal size and one face cloth size. Many hostels do not provide towels and often charge an extra fee for one. In addition to a bath towel, it is handy to have a small towel to

bring into the bathroom when you are washing up for the day or night.

- Travel bed sheet. Most hostels provide linens, but sometimes you wouldn't want to lay your head on them. It is handy to have a personal sheet to wrap around yourself when your accommodations are questionable. You can buy a travel 'cocoon' that folds down to nothing and can wrap up your whole body.
- Ear plugs and eye mask. Saviors for dorm life.
- Bungee cord and carabineers. These come in handy for packing and any MacGyver-ing you may need to do.
- Small flashlight.
- Hat. Great for sun protection and being more 'incognito'; also a nice way to represent where you are from and can serve as a conversation starter
- Hiking boots.
- Flip flops. Not only for the beach, but also essential for hostel shower use!
- Sneakers.
- Versatile clothing. Quick dry clothing that is neutral/dark in color and that can be layered, mixed, and matched is great for a backpacking trip. The layering part comes in handy for various climates. White clothing is always a bad idea! It shows dirt and can get ruined easily.
- Toiletries. Starting a trip with travel size shampoo, conditioner, soap, and toothpaste is a good move. You don't need to pack more than one set of this stuff, though, as these items can be purchased along the way and you don't want to add weight where you don't need to. A word to the wise for the ladies—tampons can be hard to come by in

certain countries. If you can't handle the thought of pads, you may want to stockpile some compact-size tampons!

- Travel makeup kit.
- Local currency. Get some in advance from your bank so that you have something to hit the ground running with. Don't get so much that you would be in a bad place if you were robbed, but get enough so that you can grab a meal, a taxi, and a night of lodging while you figure out the local cash situation.
- Emergency stash of US dollars. This is good to have to get that black-market exchange rate on the street where applicable (and just because)! Depending on economic conditions, USD can be very highly valued and can give you some bargaining power. Again, you don't want to bring too much, because getting robbed is a real possibility! I carried around $250.00 with me in a money belt to start.
- Money belt. This is a money carrying device of sorts that can be strapped around your body (under your clothes) to hold your valuables in case your backpack and/or purse is stolen.
- Inflatable pillow.

Travel documents

Many countries require at least six months of remaining passport validity to enter. Check your passport's expiration date and the amount of free space you have left in the pages. Processing a new passport request can take three to six weeks, so it's important to do this early.

Bring copies of your passport so that you can leave your

actual passport locked up while out and about in different places. Leave copies with friends and family at home as well. Other important documents include: vaccination cards/proof, immunization history report, travel insurance confirmation, spare passport photos for use in obtaining visas.

Other things to consider

When embarking on any long-term travel or move, you need to remember to change your address and/or forward your mail to someone you can rely on. I forwarded my mail to my mother and gave her a checkbook of mine, as I trusted her to manage any bills that may have come along.

You should also change your ATM pin to four digits if you have a longer pin. Many international ATMs will not accept a longer pin (I learned this the hard way). Notify your bank and credit card companies of your travel plans so your cards don't get shut off.

Planning the actual travel part

I purposely avoided planning too much of my actual trip, but your desires may differ. As I mentioned, I booked three nights in a hostel for the very beginning so that I would have a destination upon arrival. I read Tripadvisor and other reviews and looked at the location when determining where to stay. While I didn't have a detailed itinerary for my trip, I had an idea of what I wanted to do so that I could research potential destinations.